European Capital Markets: Towards a
General Theory of International
Investment

European Capital Markets

Towards a General Theory of International Investment

Bruno H. Solnik
Stanford University

Lexington Books
D.C. Heath and Company
Lexington, Massachusetts
Toronto   London

Library of Congress Cataloging in Publication Data

Solnik, B. H.
    European capital market.

    Bibliography: p.
      1. Investments, Foreign. 2. Investments–
Mathematical models. I. Title.
HG4538.S519   332.6'73   73-6594
ISBN 0-669-87064-1

Table of Contents

v

List of Tables and Figures

Tables

Figures

Preface

In this book I attempt to describe a theoretical foundation of the analysis of international portfolio investment and the efficiency of competitive capital markets in allocating the risk of return from investment among individuals across the world.

During the past few years a number of people have contributed to the formulation of a strong theoretical framework to the study of the capital market. This is generally referred to as "modern capital market theory." However, this analysis is far from being complete and is conducted in a purely domestic framework with the market isolated from the rest of the world. Therefore it doesn't integrate the international dimension and its specific characteristics. This is a fundamental drawback to this analysis, especially when international monetary events keep reminding us of the strong dependence of any economic policy, even domestic, on international flows of capital. With international trade, investment, and speculation constantly growing and becoming of such importance to a domestic economy, the international dimension of investing in capital markets cannot be neglected.

I have attempted to draw a general theory of international investment in capital markets, taking into account exchange risk, which is the added dimension of foreign investment.

Up to now most studies of international capital flows have been concerned with flows between two countries, isolated from the rest of the world. They also failed to employ the rigorous, modern tools of economic analysis developed by other authors in their contribution to modern capital market theory.

Also speculation (or investment) in foreign exchange has traditionally been considered in isolation from investment in capital market. This book will try to integrate both aspects in an equilibrium model of the world capital market; therefore it will consider explicitly the tradeoff between return and risk in foreign exchange.

There will no doubt be many who will find this book too theoretical and abstract. I believe, however, that each should be able to approach his personal investment decision more effectively by seeing it in a perspective provided by a coherent theoretical framework. In addition, some very practical conclusions for investment strategies are derived in this text.

I owe a special debt to Professor Alain Cotta of the University of Paris, who awakened my interest in economic analysis. Most of this work has been accomplished during my doctoral studies at the Massachusetts Institute of Technology. I have benefitted greatly from my association with Professor Franco Modigliani, who has been a constant source of inspiration for my research. This work would not have been possible without the unfailing help and friendship of Professor Gerald Pogue. I also greatly appreciated the constant advice and support of Professors Robert Merton, Stewart Myers, and Myron Scholes. My colleagues at Stanford University, Professors William Sharpe, Alan Kraus, Robert Litzenberger, and John McDonald, kindly read and criticized parts of an earlier draft.

Finally, I must thank my wife Catherine for her patience. However, this is only a normal compensation for what I had to endure when she was writing her own medical book.

1 Introduction: Towards an International Capital Market

Many of the existing studies in international finance are based on a segmented market approach that considers the different national capital markets as independent entities. Different currency areas, separated political organizations, and trade barriers are usually taken as a priori justification for a segmented approach to the analysis of international capital markets.

However, the development of international investment is evidenced by the rapidly growing share of foreign investors in Wall Street and various nonAmerican markets. Similarly, a large number of foreign stocks are being listed on the official exchanges of many countries, providing the investors with an easy way to obtain international diversification. Also, in many countries institutional investors have offered international mutual funds to the public (e.g., the French SICAV).

The purpose of this book is to develop an equilibrium model of the international capital market, and to test the hypothesis that security price behavior is consistent with a single world market concept. In Part I an equilibrium model of the international capital market will be developed in the capital asset pricing model framework. Since this theory is based on the assumption that there are no constraints on international capital flows, arguments in favor of a growing internationalization of equity markets are presented later in this chapter.

A fundamental dimension of this international market is the existence of exchange risk and mechanisms providing protection to investors unwilling to carry that kind of risk. In Chapter 2 forward exchange contracts are described in a formulation consistent with our framework. While some of the traditional results are found, this enables us to integrate exchange risk in the theoretical model.

The international asset pricing model is presented in Chapter 3. Some "mutual funds theorems" can be derived with important implications for investment policies. Similarly, risk pricing relations are derived from the demand clearing equations for bonds and stocks.

In Chapter 4 the real world validity of such a model is questioned and various imperfections of international markets are presented which limit the applicability of this theory. This model is tested in Part II, using statistics for

1

230 European securities and a sample of American securities. The international pricing of risk is especially investigated.

A brief review of the literature on the empirical studies on international equity markets is given in Chapter 5. The data used in this study are then described in Chapter 6.

Several stochastic security price processes are consistent with this model. Two different specifications of the testable relation between return and risk are investigated. Therefore we not only test the international pricing relation but also investigate the international capital market structure and the relationship between security prices of different countries. In Chapter 7, a single world index model is used to test the IAPM, using national and international diversified portfolios.

This type of single international index specification is discussed in Chapter 8, and some multinational index models are introduced.

Finally, Chapter 9 is a summary and an attempt to develop conclusions and implications beyond those reported in earlier chapters.

The Emergence of an International Capital Market

Several factors suggest the emergence of an international equity market and support the assumptions made by this book. Let us investigate some of these points.

In the past decade, international capital flows have increased in large pro-portions. Although official statistics are not very adequate for the analysis of capital flows,[1] they show a definite trend in international portfolio investment. Portfolio investment is distinguished from direct investment by the investor's holding share of stock in a corporation. Even though the portfolio investor may be entitled to vote his shares of stock, he plays a negligible role in the affairs of the corporation. On the other hand, the basic definition of direct investment runs in term of control. In this study we are only interested in the portfolio motive.

In the U.S., for example, the official foreign net purchase of American shares traded in Wall Street has jumped from a yearly average of $200 million in the '50s and early '60s to more than 2.5 billion dollars in the past few years. Purchase of American residents of foreign stocks (traded on the NYSE) have increased similarly as it can be seen in Figure 1-1. Foreign investors have always played a more important role on the European stock markets than on the U.S. market.[2] However since 1969, foreign purchases and sales taking place on some

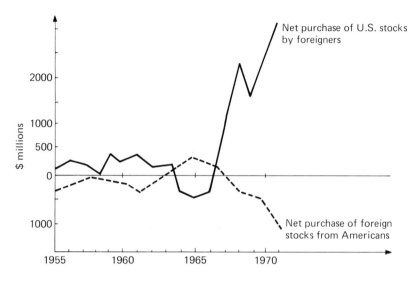

Figure 1-1. Foreign demand.

markets have been so large compared to the total volume of transactions that it can swamp the market, thereby damaging the economy and persuading many that the best solution is total isolation.

Even if very protectionist measures have been taken on an emergency basis, the general trend among governments is towards an internationalization of their stock exchanges. The recent development of international capital flows shows that such a liberalization is in great demand among investors.

Another factor facilitating international investment is the listing of foreign securities on domestic markets. Table 1-1 gives a summary of the number of foreign securities listed on major stock markets. Extensive foreign listing is present in Belgium, France, Netherlands, Switzerland, and the U.K., and to a certain extent in Germany. Also internationally diversified mutual funds are starting to be offered to residents of many countries (French SICAV).

The need for a wider lending and borrowing market, without most of the controls, constraints, and tax obstacles that characterized some domestic markets, has inspired the rapid development of the Eurodollar and Eurobond markets. These markets are quite efficient and have helped to narrow the interest rates differential in the world. There is little doubt that this loan and bond market is truly international and it should help the eventual emergence of a world equity market.

The determined action of international institutions such as the EEC [8] and

Table 1-1
Number of Security Issues Traded in 1966

	Shares		Bonds	
	Domestic	Foreign	Domestic	Foreign
Austria (Vienna)	96	0	136	2
Belgium (Brussels)	489	146	307	6
Canada (major markets)		1,872		
France (Paris)	1,180	457[1]	1,312	435[1]
Germany				
(all official markets)	618	27	3,223	35
Italy (Milan)				
official market	137	0	364	0
unofficial market	128	0	–	0
Japan (all markets)				
official markets	1,593	0	28	0
unofficial markets	106	0	259	0
Netherlands (Amsterdam)[2]				
official market	602	351	1,025	261
unofficial market	248	0	266	17
Sweden (Stockholm)				
official market	153	0	634	18
unofficial market	33	13	–	0
Switzerland (Zürich)	112	74	634	190
United Kingdom (London)[3]	5,880[4]	636[4]	2,348	567
United States (all markets)	2,937	130	1,331	

[1] Including the Overseas Franc Area.
[2] End 1966.
[3] March 1966.
[4] Estimate.

Sources: France: "Année boursière"; Japan: Ministry of Finance, United States: Securities and Exchange Commission; all other countries: Central Banks.

Note: These are the statistics at the beginning of the period used for the empirical study.

the OECD [28] and [30] is also an important factor in the creation of coherent relations among national markets. The short term goals for the Common Market is the harmonization of quotation techniques, taxes, and exchange regulations among the various countries, coupled with a more extensive listing of foreign securities.

As a final remark, it should be stressed that financial institutions still assume the bulk of international investment. But this by no means denies the existence of an efficient international market. Thus, there might be a sufficient number of active worldwide investors to create a competition that will ensure the existence of a world market, taking into account the international characteristics of securities—especially as far as risk is concerned. The following theory is based on this assumption.

Notes

1. See a discussion of this point and some statistics up to 1966 in the European Economic Community report: "The Development of a European Capital Market," 1966 [7] in the Bibliography.
2. See Donald Templeman [36].

**Part I
An Equilibrium Model of the International
Capital Market**

2 Exchange Risk

When considering an international market, a fundamental dimension should be added to the anslysis: the exchange risk. Anyone investing abroad will bear not only the risk due to the real characteristics of the investment but also an exchange risk. In recent years all currencies have been widely fluctuating and large profits obtained in a foreign country can be nullified by changes in parities.

Capital gains and losses expressed in terms of an annual rate of return on the invested sum are very sensitive to even small changes in the exchange rate. Consider the case where the sterling is bought at 2.79 but can be sold for only 2.77 just one month later, when the short term investment matures. This is equivalent to a loss of 8.4 percent per year on the invested capital. Thus it can be seen that the foreign placement of funds in the fashion described here is quite risky and bears a strong element of speculation. Some investors might be unwilling to bear this kind of risk and there must be a means of removing the investment from the realm of speculation. The market for forward exchange provides such a means.

Since the concept of exchange risk is central to international investment, the next pages will deal with the mechanisms involved in exchange risk coverage and its integration in the theoretical framework to be developed later.

Exchange Risk Coverage

There are two ways a foreigner investing on the American security market can be "covered"[1] : (1) he can go to the forward exchange market and enter a contract to deliver an amount of dollars equivalent to its investment at a given date; or (2) he can borrow dollars on the American market (or Eurodollar market) and sell them immediately (i.e., exchange them for his own currency at the spot rate). In turn he can invest them in his own country bond.

While the forward market is typically used for short term investment protection or speculation (90 days or less), the second method is more adapted to portfolio investment. In the case of equity investment, where the final return is uncertain, the protection only holds at the first approximation.

Traditionally three different types of foreign investments are considered:

pure investment, interest arbitrage, and speculation. Although this separation is questionable, these three types of foreign investment will be briefly reviewed and formulated in a mean variance framework so that it can be integrated in this model.

Pure Investment or Hedging

Pure investors are traders and investors who do not wish to bear exchange risk. For instance, exporters might want to cover a claim on a Brazilian buyer or, vice versa, an importer might want to cover the bill he will have to pay in a foreign currency upon delivery. All these people use the two techniques outlined above.

Let μ_{ik} be the expected change in parity[a] of currency i relative to currency k.

d_{ik} be the cost or rate of coverage (in % of investment)

$$d_{ik} = \frac{\text{[forward price of currency } i \text{ in terms of } k] - \text{[today's spot price]}}{\text{[today's spot price]}}$$

For various reasons it is often asserted that forward exchange rates are biased estimates of future exchange rates. This relation will be investigated in some detail later on in our theory of international capital markets.

Interest Arbitragers

Interest differentials among various countries will generally result in short term capital movements. Typically, banks will invest in foreign marketplaces, where the yield is higher than on their domestic market. But if these banks were just buying foreign currencies to invest them in risk free bonds, they would assume exchange risk. The gain realized on the interest differential, which is generally small, could be more than offset by exchange rate fluctuations. Interest arbitragers rarely take that risk and get automatic coverage on the forward market.

---

[a]μ_{ik} is not the forecasted value of the change but it is the mathematical expected value for the investment period concerned; e.g., if one considers a devaluation of 12% as equally likely anytime in the next 3 months, the expected change in parity for a one-month investment is 1/3 of 12%, or 4%.

In equilibrium one would expect that the coverage cost (in percent of initial amount) would exactly equal the interest rate differential.

$$R_k - R_i = d_{ik} \qquad\qquad (1)$$

where

R_i is the interest rate of country i,

R_k is the interest rate of country k,

d_{ik} is the coverage cost (in percent).

This relation should hold, since any investor looking for a *riskless* investment has the opportunity of either investing in the bond of his own country getting R_k or exchanging currency to invest in the bond of another country (R_i) while buying a forward contract (d_{ik}) to repatriate his investment and profit at a fixed rate. The relation $R_k - R_i = d_{ik}$ has to hold, otherwise a perfect arbitrage would exist. However this would only be the case in a world of perfect markets with equal lending and borrowing rates and no exchange controls.

Besides, flow adjustments make these differentials temporary. Interest rates are not very sensitive to interest arbitrage operations up to a certain point, since they result from a much larger volume of domestic transactions and are often set by national governments. Similarly, the currency spot rate is stable and set by a large volume of trade transaction and government actions. Therefore the forward exchange rate will principally adjust to the other three factors to restore equilibrium. Since we are concerned with equilibrium conditions and perfect markets, it will be assumed that no perfect arbitrage is possible,[b] that is:

$$R_k - R_i = d_{ik}$$

Speculation

A speculator is an investor who exposes himself deliberately to the risk of uncertainty in future exchange prices. By taking definite views on what these prices will be, he expects to make profit. His objectives are just opposite (thus complementary) to those of the covered investor. Another way to speculate is just to hold, on purpose, a foreign currency.

---

[b]This is a traditional result in forward exchange theory.

How can a forward contract be described analytically? Following are two ways.

1. Let us assume that an investor from country k decides to buy his own currency k forward—i.e., he buys a contract to purchase currency k with currency i at a fixed date. The cost of coverage is d_{ik} (the change in exchange rate expressed in percent). d_{ik} can be positive or negative; then the expected gain on this transaction is $d_{ik} - \mu_{ik}$.

The speculator can invest, in the meantime, in the risk free asset of country k up to the date of the forward contract. The total risk of such an operation will be the exchange of risk φ_{ik}:

$$\tilde{R} = R_k + d_{ik} - \tilde{m}_{ik}$$
$$E(R) = R_k + d_{ik} - \mu_{ik}$$
$$\sigma^2 = \text{variance of } \tilde{m}_{ik} = \varphi_{ik}$$

	Today	Maturity
Country k	0	t

Country i $\xrightarrow{\hspace{1em} R_k \hspace{1em}}$

$$\mu_{ik} \downarrow \uparrow d_{ik}$$

For example, assume an American investor (country k) selling forward French francs for U.S. dollars. Today's spot rate is $100 for ^{F}500; the three-month forward rate is $\$(100)(1 + d_{ik})$ for ^{F} 500 (if $d_{ik} > 0$ the dollar sells at a discount). In three months he will buy 500 FF at the spot rate of $100 (1 + \tilde{m}_{ik})$ and deliver them to get $100 (1 + d_{ik})$ as agreed in his forward contract.

He will profit if $100 (1 + \tilde{m}_{ik}) < 100 (1 + d_{ik})$. His profit per dollar is $d_{ik} - \tilde{m}_{ik}$.

2. If the speculator was instead selling his own currency forward, this contract could similarly be described as:

$$\tilde{R} = R_k + \tilde{m}_{ik} - d_{ik}$$
$$E(\tilde{R}) = R_k + \mu_{ik} - d_{ik}$$
$$\sigma^2(R) = \varphi_{ik}$$

and schematically

	Time 0	Time t

Country k $\xrightarrow{\hspace{2cm} R_k \hspace{2cm}}$

Country i $d_{ik} \downarrow \uparrow \mu_{ik}$

Identically, the same investor from country k could have exchanged his currency for currency i at the spot rate (time 0), invested it in the risk free assets of country i (yielding R_i) and converted it into his currency k at the end of the period. This operation could be described as:

$$\tilde{R} = R_i + \tilde{m}_{ik}$$
$$E(\tilde{R}) = R_i + \mu_{ik}$$
$$\sigma^2(\tilde{R}) = \varphi_{ik}$$

	Time 0	Time t

Country k

Country i $\xrightarrow{\hspace{2cm} R_i \hspace{2cm}}$ μ_{ik}

$$R_i + \mu_{ik} = R_k + \mu_{ik} - d_{ik}$$

therefore

$$d_{ik} = R_k - R_i$$

This relation implies that both types of coverage should be identical. The left-hand side represents the "cost" in the forward market while the righthand side represents the coverage "cost" of hedging. Since the two contracts are identical we will only use the second type of contract: going short in the risk free asset of the foreign country and long in the investor's risk free asset.

Conclusions

The formulation of a pure exchange risk contract will be used in the equilibrium model of the next chapter. However it will be shown that the traditional

separation between pure investors and speculators is rather arbitrary and unwarranted.

Notes

1.   See Grubel [14] and Kindleberger [22].

3 The International Asset Pricing Model

One of the more important developments of modern capital theory is the Sharpe-Lintner-Mossin mean variance equilibrium model of exchange, commonly called the "capital asset pricing model."[1]

This model applied to a single national market suggests that all investors could make their investment decisions by choosing their portfolios from two funds: the market portfolio and the risk free asset. Besides, the model predicts that the expected extra return from holding an asset is proportional to the co-variance of its return with the market portfolio (its "beta"). With a less restrictive set of assumptions, Merton [28], [29] has developed an intertemporal equilibrium model of the capital market. The intertemporal nature of this model allows it to capture effects that would never appear in a static model.

The same type of framework will be used to develop a theory of an international capital market, therefore the developments already pesented in Merton [29] will be described more briefly here.

Even the intertemporal capital asset pricing model has important limitations because it only considers national investment. Therefore this theory can only hold in a completely segmented world capital market. It is not true that it could be extended by simply including foreign investment opportunities in the market portfolio; this model would not represent a general equilibrium and would lose all economic substance and appeal. As a matter of fact, very few attempts have been made to use this kind of approach to develop an international equilibrium model of the capital markets.[a]

Among the various complexities of such a task are the nonexistence of a universal risk free asset (and different interest rates) and the presence of exchange risk, which alters the characteristics of the same investment from different countries. Possible change in parities imply that a same asset might yield different returns (and therefore different expectations on returns) for citizens of different countries. In a mean variance framework the investment opportunity set facing investors from various countries will vary, even in a perfect and integrated inter-

---

[a]See for example Grubel [15]. Most of the work published is concerned with the investment behavior of citizens of *one* given country facing an enlarged investment opportunity set.

15

national capital market. The model developed below will attempt to deal with these problems in designing an equilibrium model of the international demand for capital assets.

International Capital Market Structure

A certain number of general assumptions have to be made about the capital market structure; they are mostly the standard assumptions of market perfection.[b]

Assumptions

A-1. The capital markets are always in equilibrium (i.e., there is no trading at nonequilibrium prices).
A-2. Standard assumptions of perfection of capital markets:
    a.   There are no transaction costs, taxes, or problems with indivisibility of assets.
    b.   There are a sufficient number of investors with a comparable level of wealth so that investors believe that they can buy or sell as much of an asset as they want at the market price.
A-3. Short sales of all assets are allowed.
A-4. In each country there exists a market (bond) for borrowing and lending at the same rate (however this rate does not have to be the same in all countries).
A-5. Trading in assets and currencies takes place continuously in time.
A-6. Investors hold homogeneous expectations about exchange rate variations and the distribution of returns in terms of the asset currency.
A-7. There are no constraints on international capital flows.
A-8. Investors' consumption is limited to their home country.

Assumptions A-1 and A-4 are the standard perfect market assumptions and their merits have been discussed extensively in the literature. Such a model of international market cannot be constructed without costs, and the doubtful assumption of homogeneous expectations (A-6) has to be made here as well. As explained by Merton, A-5 follows directly from A-2. If there are no costs to transacting, and assets can be exchanged on any scale, then investors would pre-

---

[b]Since most of these assumptions are common to the capital asset pricing model and have been discussed extensively, the formulation proposed by Merton [29] will be used here.

fer to be able to revise their portfolios at any time (whether they actually do so or not).

The last two points summarize all the assumptions on international behavior and market structure. A-7 is central to this model. As far as the consumption pattern of investors is concerned, A-8 implies a strict national separation but does not forbid buying foreign goods with the local currency. This assumption will be discussed in more detail on page 19.

Rates of Return Dynamics and Exchange Rate Structure

It is assumed that expectations in real terms are homogeneous across all investors and that the price dynamics are described[c] by:

$$\frac{dI_i}{I_i} = \alpha_i dt + \sigma_i dz_i \qquad i = 1, 2, \ldots, n$$

where

$\dfrac{dI_i}{I_i}$ is the instantaneous rate of return on the market portfolio of country i[d]

α_i is the instantaneous expected rate of return

σ_i is the instantaneous standard deviation

dz_i is the standard Gauss Wiener process with zero mean

We also assume the existence of risk free asset B_i in each country:

$$\frac{dB_i}{B_i} = R_i dt$$

---

[c]For a discussion of and further references to stochastic differential equations of this type, see Merton [28] and [29].

[d]*Notation:* When the index k appears as a *subscript* it refers to a country k or its assets; when the index κ appears as a *superscript* it refers to a typical investor of country k (investor *kappa* of country k).

For simplicity of notation, only one asset per country (the market portfolio) will be considered. However, it will be seen that investment decisions reduce the choice to market portfolios, not individual assets; identical results would be found if one started with all individual assets. Unfortunately, the notational crisis would be unsolvable.

Where R_i is the risk free rate of country i.

For the time being we will further make the assumption that the investment opportunity set is constant through time, (i.e., α_i, σ_i, R_i constant). This implies that the distributions of asset prices will be lognormal. Let us call f_{ik} the exchange rate between country i and country k. Then with the same assumptions[e]

$$\frac{df_{ik}}{f_{ik}} = \mu_{ik}dt + \varphi_{ik}dq_{ik}$$

where

μ_{ik} is the expected change of parity, φ_{ik} is its standard deviation.

Then for an investor κ from country k, the instantaneous return on an investment in country i will by (by Itô lemma):

$$\frac{dI_i^\kappa}{I_i^\kappa} = \frac{d(f_{ik}I_i)}{f_{ik}I_i} = \frac{df_{ik}}{f_{ik}} + \frac{dI_i}{I_i} + \frac{df_{ik}}{f_{ik}} \times \frac{dI_i}{I_i}$$

$$\frac{dI_i^\kappa}{I_i^\kappa} = (\mu_{ik} + \alpha_i + \rho_{ik}\sigma_i\varphi_{ik})\,dt + \sigma_i dz_i + \varphi_{ik}dq_{ik}$$

where

ρ_{ik} represents the correlation coefficient between changes in the exchange rate f_{ik} and the returns on the asset i.

$\Sigma = \|\sigma_{ij}\|_{nxn}$ will denote the covariance matrix of assets returns (on real terms)

$\Phi^k = \|\Phi_{ij}^k\|$ will denote the covariance matrix of exchange rates, for
$n-1xn-1$ country k

---

[e]A characteristic of foreign exchange is the existence of a forward market, which allows the investor to cover his foreign investment. We have seen earlier how such a forward contract can be described in a mean variance framework and that it is equivalent to going short in the risk free asset of the foreign country (a well-known result). Therefore the present model does consider the existence of a forward market and the possibility of covering exchange risk.

i.e., $\Phi_{ij}^k = \text{cov}(\tilde{m}_{ik}, \tilde{m}_{jk})$ covariance of change of parity of currency i (relative to k) with change of parity of currency j (relative to k)

If, for example, a devaluation is expected on currency i relative to currency k then μ_{ik} should be negative.

Preference Structure and Budget Equation Dynamic

Consider a world economy with n countries. Each consumer κ (of country k) is supposed to maximize his expected utility, given his current wealth, the states variables of the investment opportunity set, and the distribution of his age of death.

In a continuous time model this expected–utility–maximization can be written as:

$$\text{Max } E_0 [\int_0^{T^\kappa} U^\kappa(C^\kappa(s),s)\, ds + B^\kappa [W^\kappa(T^\kappa),T^\kappa]\,] \qquad (2)$$

where $U^\kappa(\ )$ is the instantaneous utility function of investor κ; it is a function of time and the instantaneous consumption flow. Both U^κ and B^κ, the bequest or utility-of-terminal-wealth function are supposed to be strictly concave Von Neumann-Morgenstern utility functions.

$W^\kappa(t)$ is the wealth of investor κ at time t, T^κ is the distribution for his age of death. $C^\kappa(t)$ is the instantaneous consumption flow.[f]

We can write the accumulation function for the κth investor of country k as:

$$dW^\kappa = W^\kappa \sum_{i=1}^n w_i^\kappa \frac{dI_i^k}{I_i^k} + W^\kappa \sum_{i=1}^n v_i^\kappa \frac{dB_i^k}{B_i^k} + (Y^\kappa - C^\kappa)dt \qquad (3)$$

where

---

[f] Because we are primarily interested in finding equilibrium conditions for the asset markets, the model assumes a single consumption good in *each* country. The model could be generalized by making C^κ a vector and introducing the relative prices as state variables. While the analysis would be similar to the one-good case, there would be systematic effects on the portfolio demands reflecting hedging behavior against unfavorable shifts in relative, consumption goods prices (i.e., in the consumption opportunity set).

Y^κ is the wage income of investor κ (of country k)

w_i^κ is the proportion of wealth invested in country i stocks

v_i^κ is the proportion of wealth invested in bonds of country i (risk free asset)

therefore,

$d_i^\kappa = w_i^\kappa W^\kappa$ is the demand for stocks of country i by investor κ

In an intertemporal equilibrium model it is not generally possible to assume, at the same time, randomness in investment returns, consumption prices and income. We will make the simplifying assumption that wage incomes are known for certain.[g] Substituting $(dI_i^k)/(I_i)$ and $(dB_i^k)/(B_i)$ in (3) we obtain:

$$\frac{dW^\kappa}{W^\kappa} = \sum_{i=1}^{n} [w_i^\kappa(\mu_{ik} + \alpha_i + \rho_{ik}\sigma_i\varphi_{ik})dt + v_i^\kappa(R_i + \mu_{ik})dt]$$

$$+ \sum_{i=1}^{n} [w_i^\kappa(\sigma_i dz_i + \varphi_{ik}dq_{ik}) + v_i^\kappa \varphi_{ik}dq_{ik}] + \frac{1}{W^\kappa}(Y^\kappa - C^\kappa)dt \quad (4)$$

with $\sum_i (w_i^\kappa + v_i^\kappa) = 1$

Let us transform the variables

$x_i^\kappa = w_i^\kappa$

$y_i^\kappa = v_i^\kappa + w_i^\kappa.$

This linear transformation will greatly simplify the algebra and is intuitively appealing:

$$w_i^\kappa I_i + v_i^\kappa B_i = x_i^\kappa(I_i - B_i) + y_i^\kappa B_i$$

---

[g]If we assume that there is no inflation (or as a matter of fact non-stochastic inflation), exchange rates can be defined as relative prices of national consumption goods. If stochastic inflation rates are taken into account, only real prices will enter in the individual utility functions; therefore, only real returns, $(dI_i)/(I_i)$ matter. The change of parity to be considered, $(dfik)/(fik)$ would result of both the difference of inflation rates between two countries and changes in relative prices. Therefore this formulation is quite general in dealing with inflation.

This transformation corresponds exactly to the exchange risk hedging or coverage described earlier:

$$x_i^\kappa (I_i - B_i)$$

indicates an investment in country i protected against exchange risk by borrowing in that same country;

$$y_i^\kappa B_i$$

indicates a speculative position in currency of country i. Finally, by replacing $y_k^\kappa = 1 - \sum\limits_{i \neq k} y_i^\kappa$, we get:

$$\frac{dW^\kappa}{W^\kappa} = \left[\sum_{i=1}^{n} x_i^\kappa (\alpha_i - R_i + \rho_{ik}\sigma_i\varphi_{ik}) + R_k + \sum_{i \neq k} y_i^\kappa (R_i + \mu_{ik} - R_k) \right] dt$$

$$+ \sum_{i \neq k} y_i^\kappa \varphi_{ik} dq_{ik} + \sum_{i=1}^{n} x_i^\kappa \sigma_i dz_i + \frac{1}{W^\kappa}(Y^\kappa - C^\kappa)dt \qquad (5)$$

The Equation of Optimality: The Demand for Assets

Let us consider the case of independence between exchange and market risks ($\rho_{ik} = 0$). This greatly simplifies the exposition while retaining the basic structure of the phenomena. The results derived in the general case can be found in Appendix A.

To simplify the exposition it will temporarily be assumed that the *expected* change in parities is zero ($\mu_{ik} = 0$). This constant term does not in any way affect the derivations and it will appear in the final results when appropriate.

Let's define $J^\kappa(\cdot)$:

$$J^\kappa(W^\kappa, t) = \max E_t [\int_t^{T^\kappa} U^\kappa(C^\kappa, s)ds + B^\kappa(W^\kappa, T^\kappa)]$$

It can be shown[h] that the necessary optimality conditions for an investor who

---

[h]Merton [29].

acts according to (2) in choosing his consumption-investment program are that, at each point of time

$$0 = \underset{(C^{\kappa}, x_i^{\kappa}, y_i^{\kappa})}{\text{Max}} \left\{ U^{\kappa}(c^{\kappa}, t) + J_W^{\kappa} [W^{\kappa} \sum_{i \neq k} y_i^{\kappa}(R_i - R_k) \right.$$

$$+ W^{\kappa} \sum_{i=1}^{n} x_i^{\kappa}(\alpha_i - R_i) + R_k] + \frac{1}{2} J_{WW}^{\kappa} [\sum_i \sum_j y_i^{\kappa} y_j^{\kappa} \Phi_{ij}^{k} (W^{\kappa})^2$$

$$\left. + \sum_i \sum_j x_i^{\kappa} x_j^{\kappa} \sigma_{ij} (W^{\kappa})^2] \right\} \tag{6}$$

Necessary conditions[i] for (6) are:

$$0 = \frac{\partial U^{\kappa}}{\partial C^{\kappa}} - J_W^{\kappa} \tag{7-a}$$

$$0 = J_W^{\kappa}(R_i - R_k) + J_{WW}^{\kappa} W^{\kappa} \sum_{j \neq k} y_j^{\kappa} \Phi_{ij}^{k} \qquad \begin{matrix} i = 1, \ldots, n \\ i \neq k \end{matrix} \tag{7-b}$$

$$0 = J_W^{\kappa}(\alpha_i - R_i) + J_{WW}^{\kappa} W^{\kappa} \sum_{j=1}^{n} x_j^{\kappa} \sigma_{ij} \qquad i = 1, \ldots, n \tag{7-c}$$

Relation (7-a) is the usual intertemporal envelope condition to equate the marginal utility of current consumption to the marginal utility of wealth (future consumption). The reader familiar with the single-period capital asset-pricing model will have recognized the similarity of relations (7-c) with the standard CAPM results.

From (7) we get:

$$\boxed{\begin{aligned} R_i - R_k &= A^{\kappa} \sum_{j \neq k} y_j^{\kappa} \Phi_{ij}^{k} \\ \alpha_i - R_i &= A^{\kappa} \sum_j x_j^{\kappa} \sigma_{ij} \end{aligned}} \tag{8}$$

---

[i]For a proof of this derivation see Merton [29]; this assumes that the income is constant or deterministic. J_W^{κ} and J_{WW}^{κ} are the first and second derivative of $J^{\kappa}(\ )$.

where

$$A^\kappa = -\frac{W^\kappa((\partial^2 J^\kappa)/(\partial W^2))}{(\partial J^\kappa)/(\partial W)}$$

or

$$\|R_i - R_k\| = A^\kappa \Phi^k y \qquad n - 1$$

$$\|\alpha_i - R_i\| = A^\kappa \Sigma x \qquad n$$

where y and x are column vectors.

The manifest characteristic of (8) is its linearity in the portfolio demands, hence we can solve directly for these demand functions by matrix inversion:

a) demand for *stock* of country i

$$d_i^\kappa = \frac{W^\kappa}{A^\kappa} \sum_{j=1}^{n} s_{ij}(\alpha_j - R_j) \qquad\qquad (8\text{-}a)$$

where s_{ij} are elements of Σ^{-1}.

These functions are identical to the single-period CAPM demand equations except that the risk free rate R_j will vary according to the national origin of asset j.

b) demand for the risk free bond of country i

$$e_i^\kappa = \frac{W^\kappa}{A^\kappa} \sum_{j \neq k} \eta_{ij}^k (R_j - R_k) - d_i^\kappa \qquad \text{for } i \neq k \qquad (8\text{-}b)$$

where η_{ij}^k are elements of $(\Phi^k)^{-1}$

While the terms under the summation sign do not depend on the country "k" for the stocks, they do depend on k for the bonds.

Since the demand functions for stocks and bonds are separable, it is easy to see directly that the ratio of demand for risky assets (stocks) will be independent of preferences and nationality. If one had considered all countries' stocks, formula

(8-a) would have been similar with one term for each individual stock. Clearly the previous results hold.

These results suggest the following separation theorem:

Separation Theorem 1

All investors will be indifferent between choosing portfolios from the original assets or from $n + 1$ funds, where a possible choice for those funds is:

—The world stock market portfolio (hedged against exchange risk)
—The n bonds of each country.

The proportion of the risky fund invested in asset i is:

$$\sum_{j=1}^{n} s_{ij}(\alpha_j - R_j) \Big/ \sum_{j=1}^{n} \sum_{i=1}^{n} s_{ij}(\alpha_j - R_j).$$

As expected, the standard two funds theorem holds for all investors from one country; they can make their selection from two funds:

1. Their domestic risk free asset
2. A portfolio of all risky assets (including foreign bonds) whose composition depends on the investor's *nationality* (not on his preferences). This fund will vary for each country.

More About the Exchange Risk

Up to now we have not really postulated any structure for the exchange rates. However, exchange parities and their fluctuations are not completely independent since they are only price relatives. These exchange rates need to be expressed in some arbitrarily chosen units.[j] Arbitrarily pick one country as the reference country (e.g., the USA and its key currency, the dollar); let it be the nth country.

---

[j]This implies that the dimension of the exchange risk, i.e., of the exchange risk variance-covariance matrix, is of rank $n - 1$ and not n.

Call Φ the $(n-1) \times (n-1)$ matrix of exchange rate covariance relative to that reference country.

$$\Phi = \Phi^n = \begin{pmatrix} \Phi^n_{11} & \cdots & \cdots & \Phi^n_{n-1} \\ & & & \\ \vdots & & \Phi^n_{ij} & \vdots \\ & & & \\ \Phi^n_{n-1,1} & \cdots & \cdots & \Phi^n_{n-1,n-1} \end{pmatrix}$$

Again, Φ^k_{ij} represents the covariance of changes in the exchange rate of currency i (relative to currency k) with changes in the exchange rate of currency j (relative to currency k).

How can we transform Φ^k into Φ? By definition:

$$\Phi^k_{ij} = \frac{df_{ik}}{f_{ik}} \cdot \frac{df_{jk}}{f_{jk}}$$

$$\Phi^k_{ij} = \left(\frac{df_{in}}{f_{in}} - \frac{df_{kn}}{f_{kn}} \right) \left(\frac{df_{jn}}{f_{jn}} - \frac{df_{kn}}{f_{kn}} \right)$$

$$\Phi^k_{ij} = \Phi^n_{ij} - \Phi^n_{kj} - \Phi^n_{ik} + \Phi^n_{kk}$$

Thus

$$\Phi^k = H^k \Phi H^{k^T}$$

where

H^k is $(n-1) \times (n-1)$

column k

and H^{k^T} is its transpose.

Similarly we can observe that:

$$\|R_i - R_k\| = H^k \|R_i - R_n\| = H^k R \tag{9}$$

In the first set of optimality conditions we had $\|R_i - R_k\| = A^\kappa \Phi^k y$. It can be rewritten as:

$$H^k R = A^\kappa H^k \Phi H^{k^T} y \tag{10}$$

where R and Φ are *independent of the investor's preferences or citizenship* (purely technological) and y is a $(n-1)$ column vector of y_i^κ.

Since H^k is inversible, we can left multiply by $(H^k)^{-1}$ on both sides of (10) to get (11):

$$R = A^\kappa \Phi H^{k^T} y \tag{11}$$

Then

$$R = A^\kappa \Phi z^\kappa$$

where

$$z^\kappa = H^{k^T} y^\kappa$$

$$
z^\kappa =
\begin{pmatrix}
y_1^\kappa \\
y_2^\kappa \\
\cdot \\
\cdot \\
y_{k-1}^\kappa \\
y_k^\kappa - 1 \\
\cdot \\
\cdot \\
y_{n-1}^\kappa
\end{pmatrix}
$$

z^κ is equal to the excess demand (over the demand for stocks) for bonds of each country, except for bonds of the investor's country. Like x_i^κ and y_i^κ, z_i^κ is expressed in *percentage* of the total investor's wealth, keeping in mind that $1 - y_k^\kappa = \sum_{j \neq k} y_j^\kappa$. This result is extremely interesting since it implies that:

$$z^\kappa = \frac{1}{A^\kappa} \Phi^{-1} R$$

or

$$z_i^\kappa = \frac{1}{A^\kappa} \sum_{j=1}^{n-1} \eta_{ij}(R_j - R_n) \qquad \text{for all } k = 1, \dots, n-1, \tag{12}$$

where η_{ij} are the elements of Φ^{-1} and do not depend on k. Clearly the ratio z_k^κ / z_j^κ is independent of preferences and nationality. The problem, however, is that z_i^κ does not really represent the demand for bonds of country i (minus demand for stock):

$$z_i^\kappa = y_i^\kappa \quad \text{for all } i \ \textit{except } i = k \ \text{ where } z_k^\kappa = y_k^\kappa - 1$$

Similarly z_n^κ can be defined as equal to the demand for assets of country n by investor κ. Thus:

$$z_n^\kappa = y_n^\kappa = 1 - \sum_{i=1}^{n-1} y_i^\kappa$$

but

$$\sum_{i=1}^{n-1} z_i^\kappa = \sum_{i=1}^{n-1} y_i^\kappa - 1$$

therefore

$$z_n^\kappa = y_n^\kappa = -\frac{1}{A^\kappa} \sum_{i=1}^{n-1} \sum_{j=1}^{n-1} \eta_{ij}(R_j - R_n)$$

Separation Theorem 2

All investors will be indifferent between choosing portfolios from the original set of assets or from 3 funds, where a possible choice for those funds is:

1. A portfolio of all stocks hedged against exchange risk (the world market portfolio)
2. A portfolio of bonds, speculative in the exchange risk dimension[k]
3. The risk free asset of their country

The proportions of the funds invested in each asset are determined by market characteristics.

Proof: Let us build a fund which will hold a proportion δ_i in asset

$I_i - B_i$ (hedged stock) with:

$$\delta_i = \frac{\displaystyle\sum_{j=1}^{n} s_{ij}(\alpha_j - R_j)}{\displaystyle\sum_i \sum_j s_{ij}(\alpha_j - R_j)}$$

and another fund made of bonds B_i ($i = 1, \ldots, n$) in proportions δ'_i with:

$$\delta'_i = \sum_{j=1}^{n-1} \eta_{ij}(R_j - R_n) \qquad \text{for } i = 1, \ldots, n - 1$$

$$\delta'_n = -\sum_{i=1}^{n-1} \sum_{j=1}^{n-1} \eta_{ij}(R_j - R_n).$$

Let λ_i^κ be the fraction of the κth investor's wealth invested in fund i ($i = 1, 2, 3$). To prove the theorem we want to show that there exists an alloca-

---

[k]Speculative in the exchange risk dimension means that this fund does not carry any "market" risk, but purely exchange risk due to the presence of foreign bonds.

tion $(\lambda_1^K, \lambda_2^K)$ which will replicate the demand functions (8-a) and (12)[1], i.e.:

$$\lambda_1^K \delta_i + \frac{1}{A^K} \sum_{j=1}^{n} s_{ij}(\alpha_j - R_j) \qquad i = 1, 2, \ldots, n$$

$$\lambda_2^K \delta_i' = \frac{1}{A^K} \sum_{j=1}^{n-1} \eta_{ij}(R_j - R_n) \qquad i = 1, \ldots, k-1, k+1, \ldots, n-1$$

$$\lambda_2^K \delta_k' + \lambda_3^K = 1 + \frac{1}{A^K} \sum_{j=1}^{n-1} \eta_{kj}(R_k - R_n)$$

$$\lambda_2^K \delta_n' = -\frac{1}{A^K} \sum_{i=1}^{n-1} \sum_{j=1}^{n-1} \eta_{ij}(R_j - R_n). \qquad (13)$$

It can easily be seen that the allocation:

$$\lambda_1^K = \frac{1}{A^K} \sum_{i=1}^{n} \sum_{j=1}^{n} s_{ij}(\alpha_j - R_j)$$

$$\lambda_2^K = \frac{1}{A^K}$$

$$\lambda_3^K = 1$$

will satisfy (13). This demonstrates the theorem.

Intuitively, since the ratio x_i^K/x_j^K and z_i^K/z_j^K are independent of k, it appears that the following funds would be adequate:

---

[1] Since the net worth of the first two funds is zero, it will be required that $\lambda_3^K = 1$.

$$I_i - R_i \qquad B_i \qquad\qquad\qquad B_k$$

$$
\begin{array}{ccc}
\begin{bmatrix} x_1 \\ \cdot \\ \cdot \\ \cdot \\ \cdot \\ \cdot \\ \cdot \\ \cdot \\ \cdot \\ x_n \end{bmatrix}
&
\begin{array}{l}
\begin{bmatrix} z_1 \\ \cdot \\ \cdot \\ \cdot \\ z_k \\ \cdot \\ \cdot \\ \cdot \\ z_n \end{bmatrix}
\end{array}
\begin{array}{l}
= y_1 \\ \\ \\ \\ = y_k - 1 \\ \\ \\ \\ = 1 - \displaystyle\sum_{i=1}^{n-1} y_i
\end{array}
&
\boxed{1}
\end{array}
$$

Although a reference country n was arbitrarily used as a base to establish equations (11), the composition of the exchange risk speculation fund (and of the market portfolio) is *independent* of the country selected.

This three-funds theorem is in fact still a $n + 1$ funds theorem since the third fund (the risk free asset of the investor's country) will change according to the investor's nationality. However, it is a much richer theorem than separation theorem 1. The new "speculation" fund is made up of risk free bonds of all countries. Because of the symmetry of the exchange risk structure, and of the mean variance framework, this fund is the *same* for everyone. Thus any investor might invest his total wealth W^K in the risk free portfolio and pick the desired level of risk by investing in the two risky funds; these are pure market risk or exchange risk funds since their net worth is zero in both cases.[m]

No one should ever be a pure speculator or a pure investor. In this model both types of risks are considered as independent. This is the reason why only three portfolios are necessary in the separation theorem. But when he picks his desired level of risk, an investor's decision is affected only by expected returns and variances and not by qualitative differences between exchange and market risk (at least in this theory).

The Equilibrium Yield Relationship
Among Assets

Given the demand function (8-a), we now derive the equilibrium market clearing conditions for the model. Since the demand function for stocks and

---

[m]One could make the analogy with the CAPM separation theorem by considering two funds: (1) the risk-free asset B_F and (2) the market portfolio "short" $M - B_F$ (with an expected return of $\alpha_M - R_F$ and a net worth of zero).

bonds are separable, the clearing conditions can be worked out independently. The equilibrium relationship between the expected returns on an individual national asset and the expected return on the international market can be derived from these conditions.

Stocks

From (8-a) the aggregate demand function, $D_i = \sum\limits_k d_i^k$ can be written as:

$$D_i = \sum_k d_i^k = \frac{1}{A} \sum_{j=1}^{n} s_{ij}(\alpha_j - R_j) \tag{14}$$

where

$$\frac{1}{A} = \sum_k \frac{W^k}{A^k} \, .$$

If $D_i = \omega_i M$ where M is the total world market value, (14) can be transformed into:

$$\alpha_i - R_i = MA \sum_{j=1}^{n} \omega_j \sigma_{ij} \tag{15}$$

Define:

$$\alpha_m = \sum_i \omega_i \alpha_i$$

$$R_m = \sum_i \omega_i R_i$$

$$\sigma_{im} = \sum_{j=1}^{n} \omega_i \sigma_{ij} \, ,$$

then (15) is equivalent to:

$$\alpha_i - R_i = MA \, \sigma_{im}$$

Multiplying (15) by ω_i and adding

$$\alpha_m - R_m = MA \sum_{i=1}^{n} \omega_i \sigma_{im} = MA \, \sigma_m^2$$

Thus

$$\boxed{\alpha_i - R_i = \frac{\sigma_{im}}{\sigma_m^2} (\alpha_m - R_m).}$$ (16)

Theorem 3

Equation (16) states that the risk premium of a security over its national risk free rate is proportional to the risk premium of the world market over an average international bond rate:

$$\alpha_i - R_i = \frac{\sigma_{im}}{\sigma_m^2} (\alpha_m - R_m).$$

Since one can always get protected against fluctuations in exchange rates by going short in the risk free asset of the corresponding country (borrowing), it could be expected that only the expected return over that interest rate is relevant in the pricing of market risk. Because of the hedging process, this risk premium will be independent of expectations on change of parities or inflation.

In this model the risk free bond of each country plays different roles. It is the risk free asset of the country but it is also a pure exchange risk asset for foreign investors, therefore allowing investors to hedge equity investment against exchange risk by going short in the foreign bond.

If the interest rates are considered to be exogenous to the system, then the above pricing relations has important economic implications. Let us assume, for example, that a country arbitrarily decides to lower its interest rate due to internal economic considerations. Then relation (16) would tend to imply that expected returns on the stocks of that country would decline accordingly. The most obvious differences between relation (16) and the capital asset pricing model relation are:

1. The systematic risk is the *international* systematic risk, involving the co-variance of the stock return with the world market portfolio

2. R_i and R_m are in general going to be different

Bonds

In the previous derivation it has been implicitly considered that the interest rates were exogenous to the model. This could be explained by the action of national governments setting rates determined by domestic economic policy and willing to borrow (or lend) an unlimited amount of funds at this rate. However this assumption might be very questionable in an equilibrium model. We will rather make the assumption that the total demand for each national bond is zero (there is a lender for each borrower).

Let us derive the demand functions for risk free assets. The demand for bonds of country i is equal to the demand for all assets of that country minus the demand for stocks. The total demand for all assets of country i is:

$$F_i = \sum_{\substack{\text{all countries} \\ k}} \sum_{\kappa \in k} W^\kappa y_i^\kappa = \sum_{k=1}^{n} f_i^k \qquad (17)$$

where f_i^k is the demand for assets of country i by investors of country k:

$$f_i^k = \sum_\kappa W^\kappa y_i^\kappa$$

By equation (12), it is known that:

$$f_i^k = \sum_\kappa W^\kappa y_i^\kappa = \sum_\kappa W^\kappa z_i^\kappa = \sum_\kappa \frac{W^\kappa}{A^\kappa} \sum_{j=1}^{n-1} \eta_{ij}(R_j - R_n)$$

Therefore:

$$f_i^k = \frac{1}{A^k} \sum_{j=1}^{n-1} \eta_{ij}(R_j - R_n) \qquad \text{for } k \neq i$$

with

$$\frac{1}{A^k} = \sum_\kappa \frac{W^\kappa}{A^\kappa}$$

and

$$f_k^k = \sum_{\kappa \in k} W^\kappa y_k^\kappa = \sum_\kappa W^\kappa (z_k^\kappa - 1)$$

Therefore:

$$f_k^k = \frac{1}{A^k} \sum_{j=1}^{n-1} \eta_{kj}(R_j - R_n) + W_k$$

where W_i is the portfolio wealth of investors of country i.

By replacing in (17), we get:

$$F_i = W_i + \frac{1}{A} \sum_{j=1}^{n-1} \eta_{ij}(R_j - R_n) \tag{18}$$

where

$$\frac{1}{A} = \sum_{i=1}^{n} \frac{1}{A^i}$$

From the assumption of zero net demand for bonds, F_i should be equal to the demand for stocks D_i. From (14) and (18):

$$D_i = W_i + \frac{1}{A} \sum_{j=1}^{n-1} \eta_{ij}(R_j - R_n) \qquad i = 1, \ldots, n \tag{19}$$

Equation (19) gives a set of relations between the interest rates across the world as a function of the national wealth, its investment opportunities and the exchange rate relations. It is possible (if one is known) to estimate each risk free rate:

$$R_i - R_n = A \sum_{j=1}^{n-1} \Phi_{ij}(D_j - W_j) \qquad i = 1, \ldots, n-1 \tag{20}$$

$D_i - W_i$ is the net wealth invested in country i. If D_i is greater than W_i it implies a net foreign investment in that country; on the opposite, when W_i is larger than D_i, it means that investors from country i lack attractive investment opportunities in their home country and are net foreign investors. Besides:

$$\sum_i (D_i - W_i) = M - M = 0$$

where M is the total market value. Let us define ω_i' as

$$\omega_i' = \frac{(D_i - W_i)}{M}$$

$$\sum_{i=1}^{n} \omega_i' = 0$$

Then replacing in (20):

$$R_i - R_n = MA \sum_{j=1}^{n-1} \omega_i' \Phi_{ij} \qquad j = 1, \ldots, n-1$$

Define:

$$R_W = \sum_{i=1}^{n-1} \omega_i'(R_i - R_n) = \sum_{i=1}^{n} \omega_i'(R_i - R_n) = \sum_{i=1}^{n} \omega_i' R_i$$

$$\Phi_{iW} = \sum_{j=1}^{n-1} \omega_j' \Phi_{ij}$$

$$\Phi_W^2 = \sum_{i=1}^{n-1} \omega_i' \Phi_{iW}$$

then

$$R_i - R_n = MA\,\Phi_{iW}.$$ (21)

Multiplying by ω_i and summing:

$$R_w = MA\,\Phi_W^2$$ (22)

Therefore the following relation can be derived:

$$R_i - R_n = \frac{\Phi_{iW}}{\Phi_W^2}\,R_W$$ (23)

For simplicity of exposition, no expected change of parities have been considered so far. However nonzero expected changes of parity can be easily introduced. Looking at the budget equation (5), it can be seen that μ_{ik} only appears in $R_i + \mu_{ik} - R_k$. This would transform the above relation into:

$$R_i + \mu_{in} - R_n = \frac{\Phi_{iW}}{\Phi_W^2}\,R_W$$ (24)

with still

$$\Phi_{iW} = \sum_{i=1}^{n-1} \omega_j' \Phi_{ij}$$

and[n]

$$R_W = \sum_{i=1}^{n-1} \omega_i'(R_i + \mu_{in} - R_n) = \sum_{i=1}^{n} \omega_i'(R_i + \mu_{in}).$$

---

[n]R_W is independent of n since:

$$\sum_{i=1}^{n} \omega_i'(R_i + \mu_{in}) = \sum_{i=1}^{n} \omega_i'R_i + \sum_{i=1}^{n} \omega_i'(\mu_{ik} - \mu_{nk}) = \sum_{i=1}^{n} \omega_i'R_i + \sum_{i=1}^{n} \omega_i'\mu_{ik}$$

Therefore:

$$R_W = \sum_{i=1}^{n} \omega_i'(R_i + \mu_{ik}) \text{ for any } k.$$

We can rewrite this as:

$$R_i - R_n = \mu_{ni} + \frac{\Phi_{iW}}{\Phi_W^2} R_W$$

(25)

Theorem 4

The difference between interest rates of two countries is equal to the expected change of parities between these two countries plus a term depending on exchange risk covariances:

$$R_i - R_n = \mu_{ni} + \frac{\Phi_{iW}}{\Phi_W^2} R_W$$

Comments

It has been shown in Chapter 2 that the forward rate of currency n in terms of currency i was such that the forward contract rate d_{ni} was equal to interest rate differential between two countries:

$$R_i - R_n = d_{ni}$$

(1)

The above relations imply that the forward exchange rate is a *biased* estimate of the future exchange rate. This is widely believed but generally for different and conflicting reasons. Here we demonstrate that the spread in interest rate should be equal to the expected change of parity plus a "hedging pressure" term. The premium charged is not a liquidity premium. These results are somewhat reminiscent of the "Habitat" theory if one interprets habitat as a stronger preference to hedge against changes in investment opportunities due to changes in parities.

The direction of the bias depends on the net foreign investment of each country. If a country has more tangibles than wealth (i.e., is a net importer of capital), then there is a hedging pressure of foreign investors who want to get protected against exchange risk on their equity investment in that country. To hedge their investment against exchange risk these investors will go short in the risk free bond of the country[o] (borrow), pushing the interest rate upwards. This conclusion can be derived from equation (25). At a first approximation Φ_{iW} is equivalent to its variance term:

$$\Phi_{iW} = \sum_j \omega'_j \Phi_{ij} \sim \omega'_i \Phi_i^2$$

If country i is a net importer of capital ($\omega'_i > 0$), the hedging term would imply that, *ceteris paribus*, the interest rate in country i would be larger.

The term

$$\frac{\Phi_{iW}}{\Phi_W^2} R_W$$

is the premium foreign investors have to pay to get their equity investment protected against exchange rate fluctuations. Hence it can be considered as a risk premium to speculators who provide that service. This relation (25) is very important because it outlines the determinants of the difference between any pair of interest rates. Only if all countries have a zero net foreign investment would the spread between interest rates be an unbiased estimate of the change in parity. In this case no one would want to speculate on foreign exchanges since the expected gain on change in parities will be *exactly* offset by the difference in interest rate and no risk premium would be provided for carrying the exchange risk; investors would only invest (short) in foreign bonds to hedge their equity investment. The only *contrepartie* would be local lenders.

From equation (19) it appears that the proportions of the speculative fund (Theorem 2) invested in each country bond are equal (or at least proportional) to the net capital position of the country.

$$\delta'_i = \sum_j \eta_{ij}(R_j - R_n) = A(D_i - W_i) = MA\omega'_i$$

with

$$\sum_i \delta'_i = \sum_i \omega'_i = 0$$

This speculative fund (with proportions, $\omega'_i = (\delta'_i)/(MA)$) will have an expected return of R_W.

While the market fund only depends on market value variables, this specula-

---

[o]Or buy a forward contract.

tive fund composition only depends on international comparison variables. It is independent of investors preferences.

This result shows that a zero-beta portfolio (no market risk) does not necessarily have an expected return equal to the risk free rate of the investor's country. This would be true for any portfolio of foreign bonds.

Conclusions

An intertemporal equilibrium model of the international capital market has been developed. It takes into account exchange risk and the existence of different interest rates across the world. Some "mutual funds theorems" can be derived with important implications for investment policies. The most important of these theorems states that all investors will be indifferent between choosing portfolios from the original assets or from three funds, namely:

1. A portfolio of stocks hedged against exchange risk (the market portfolio)
2. A portfolio of bonds, speculative in the exchange risk dimension
3. The risk free asset of their own country

The first two portfolios are independent of investors' preferences or citizenship.

A risk pricing relation for stocks has been derived which states that the risk premium of any security over its national risk free rate is proportional to its international systematic risk. The coefficient of proportionality is the risk premium of the world market over a world bond rate. Another set of risk pricing relations states that the difference between interest rates of two countries is equal to the expected change of parities between these two countries plus a term depending on exchange risk covariances. This implies that the forward exchange rate is a *biased* estimate of the future exchange rate.

These findings have important practical implications. They provide investors with a simple but powerful investment strategy, and they also indicate the need for internationally diversified mutual funds. As a matter of fact, a single fund invested in all common stocks (with market value weights) would satisfy the needs of investors from any country. As of now it is much easier for any national to speculate on foreign exchanges (or hedge) through his domestic forward exchange market than it is to invest in foreign common stocks.

One should keep in mind, however, that these results depend on restrictive assumptions about homogenous expectations, consumption patterns, and perfection of capital markets. The more basic and traditional criticism to the international asset pricing model would be aimed at the fundamental assumption that there are no constraints on international capital flows. While many factors suggest a growing internationalization of capital markets (see Chapter 1), there are still impediments to foreign investments. These constraints will briefly be outlined in Chapter 4.

Notes

1.   See Sharpe [36] and [38], Lintner [25], and Mossin [31].

4

Some Limitations to the Theory: Constraints on Capital Flows

The model developed here assumed market perfection and no constraint on international capital flows. However, direct restrictions or adverse incentives to international investment still exist. Let us investigate the main criticisms that could be made to the framework of our theory.

Restrictions on International Investment

The Motivations

Leaving aside the current state of exchange control measures introduced since 1972, countries have historically maintained exchange controls or impediments to capital movements for three reasons:

1. Balance-of-payments protection.
2. Domestic capital market protection, i.e., domestic savings are inadequate to meet existing domestic investment demand.
3. Investor protection, i.e., the central government believes it must protect the interest of its residents in its own market, and, more rarely, in their transactions in foreign markets.

Nothing in either the 1972 IMF Annual Report on Exchange Restrictions [18] or in the most recent OECD Code [34] (1969 published edition as amended to 1970) indicates that governments have taken major positive steps to stimulate either outflows of long term capital or the growth of international capital markets. When additional liberalization measures are taken, as in Japan recently, these appear to be a safety valve for the balance-of-payments position, i.e., to keep surpluses in manageable proportions. More than anything the *will* of national governments to move toward a true relaxation of restrictions and follow, for example, the recommendations of the EEC or OECD is not very evident.

The Constraints

Within the general context of capital movements there are four types of restrictions that directly affect the securities markets: exchange regulation, taxation, restricted admission of foreign securities on capital markets, and restricted buying and selling of securities.

Exchange Control. Some countries, in particular the Scandinavian countries, Spain and Portugal, and, until recently, Japan, very rigidly control portfolio investment inflows and outflows. Italy and France carefully watch portfolio capital outflows, although residents of these countries have generally been able to purchase abroad foreign listed securities. France has at times utilized a "financial franc," which has raised the price of the transactions.

U.K. residents have been able to purchase foreign securities abroad, subject to an investment dollar premium and a surrender provision of 25 percent of the foreign exchange proceeds from the sale of their foreign security holdings. One result of this latter rule was to make investment in offshore funds attractive; the offshore fund made portfolio changes on its own behalf, rather than in the name of its U.K. shareholder. There was, therefore, no surrender requirement imposed on the U.K. investor, who nonetheless was able to benefit from changes in the basic portfolio managed by the offshore funds in which he had invested. Austria, Belgium-Luxembourg, and the Netherlands are relatively liberal in permitting residents to purchase foreign securities abroad, although a special currency market exists in Belgium-Luxembourg.

Switzerland and Germany are the most liberal, with no apparent restrictions in their residents' purchases of foreign securities abroad, as distinct from the informal restrictions mentioned above on direct foreign flotations in their domestic capital markets.

Taxation. In the area of taxation, the obstacles are varied. First of all, there are general differences in taxation systems among countries that influence a borrower's choice of sources of finance and a lender's choice of investment. Secondly, there are tax instruments destined specifically to limit flows of capital to foreign countries, such as the Interest Equalization Tax in the U.S. Another important obstacle is double taxation, through the imposition of taxes by the country of source and the country of residence. This problem has widely been solved through the conclusion of bilateral double taxation treaties between industrialized countries. Nevertheless, many countries have still not concluded such agreements, and the administration of the tax credit procedure is cumbersome and complicated.

Restricted Listing. Apart from these barriers of a more general nature, many countries have erected obstacles to the admission of securities to capital markets and to exchanges.[1] One of the most carefully controlled areas is the issue of domestic securities abroad, and the issue of foreign securities on the domestic market. Many countries wish to retain a considerable degree of control over the primary (i.e., new issue) market, since new issues have an important impact on the stability of the market for raising long term capital and because of the effects of new foreign issues on domestic interest rates and on domestic monetary policy in general. These restrictions, of course, can also ultimately affect sales in the secondary market.

The admission of outstanding securities to listing or trading on exchange is subject to less restriction than new issues, but is nevertheless extensively regulated. Barriers relating to the introduction of foreign securities on domestic stock exchanges are of various types. These restrictions may take the form of prior authorization from the authorities, stamp duties, concrete form of the securities, and discrimination against unlisted securities.

Restricted Sales. Another set of obstacles which have been erected by many governments are directed against the buying and selling of securities. With regard to the purchase and sale abroad by domestic residents, of foreign securities, only one OECD country has a full reservation to the Code against the purchase and sale of listed securities; five countries have reservations against unlisted securities. Many countries have partial reservations. Here the major discrimination is between listed and unlisted securities. This distinction is becoming archaic, particularly in regard to securities registered in the U.S. where the requirements of the 1933 and 1934 Securites Exchange Acts are equally stringent for all securities offered to the public.

A second major category of restriction concerns the purchase and sale by residents of foreign securities on their own domestic market. Here again, apart from taxation and exchange regulations mentioned above, there are various administrative, legal, and other obstacles. The most important concerns investment prescriptions for financial institutions. Many countries prevent banks, insurance companies, and pension funds from purchasing listed or unlisted foreign securities. Is this sensible in a period of growing centralization and integration? In Belgium, for instance, insurance companies may not hold more than 20 percent of their reserves in foreign stocks; French insurance companies may not purchase unlisted securities, domestic or foreign. In Germany similar provisions exist for investment companies limiting acquisitions to listed foreign securities. In Italy the purchase of nonofficially listed foreign securities by banks is subject to authorization. The Netherlands and Switzerland also have rules limiting financial institutions' investments in foreign securities.

Conclusions

It is hard to evaluate the importance of these restrictions[2] on the freedom of capital movement. Clearly they do not prevent anyone from investing abroad; however, they might make the international market less efficient because of the transaction costs involved. The question is how much these restrictions affect the international pricing of securities. Even if few people have *direct* access to foreign investment, the role played by the international investors, especially financial institutions, might make the capital markets efficient and imply an international pricing of risk. This point will be investigated empirically in the next chapters.

Notes

1. The Business and Industry Advisory Committee of the OECD (BIAC) Group of Experts on Capital Markets and Capital Movements reviewed these barriers in detail in a report published in March 1969. The OECD Code of Liberalization of Capital Movements also sets forth the restrictions remaining in this field [33] and [34].
2. Because of the monetary crisis of the early 70s most countries have taken drastic measures to protect themselves against speculative international capital flows. While these measures are supposed to be merely temporary, they further restrict foreign portfolio investment.

**Part II
An Empirical Investigation of the
International Capital Market**

5

Introduction and Review of the Literature

Introduction to Part II

The international asset pricing model presented in Part I will now be tested. Based on a certain set of assumptions, this model enabled us to establish two important risk pricing relations:

1. From the demand equations for stocks, it has been possible to demonstrate that the risk premium of a security over its national risk free rate is proportional to its international systematic risk where the coefficient of proportionality is the world market risk premium over an average bond rate:

$$\alpha_i - R_i = \beta_i(\alpha_m - R_m) \tag{16}$$

2. The difference between interest rates of two countries is equal to the expected change of parities between these two countries plus a term depending on exchange risk covariances:

$$R_i - R_n = \mu_{ni} + \frac{\Phi i W}{\Phi^2 W} R_W \tag{25}$$

Since the risk pricing relations for bonds and stocks are separable, it would be possible to test them independently. However, relation (25) would be difficult to estimate since expected change in parities and exchange risk covariances would be hard to measure. (It is most likely that past data would not help so much because of the lack of stationarity.) This endeavor is left for future times and this book will focus on the examination of the risk pricing relation for stocks. stocks. The same approach is generally used to test (indirectly) the capital asset pricing model.

The purpose of this empirical part is not only to test the international asset pricing model but also to investigate the international market structure and the relationship between security prices of different countries.

Several stochastic security price processes are consistent with this model. On one side, one can postulate a perfectly integrated international capital market

47

with no national influence. This structure, a single international index model, will be specified. On the other side a very nationalistic market structure is also consistent with the international asset pricing model.

One never expects the truth to lie at extremes, so our final effort will be to investigate the relative importance of the international and national factors. It should be noted that exchange rate variations are assumed to be the only risk attached to foreign investment in addition to investment risk. Risks on foreign investment stemming from war, confiscation, and exchange restrictions could not be quantified and were disregarded. Consequently, the variances used in the subsequent calculations might understate foreign risk. The limitation of such an analysis appears clearly if one considers more unstable countries (e.g., Venezuela) where the political risk is an important determinant of the investment decision which cannot be integrated in the mean variance framework. However, this problem is not crucial for Western European and American capital markets.

Review of the Literature

As it has been outlined earlier, the traditional study of capital markets and asset prices behavior is based on a segmented approach where each national stock market is considered in isolation. Only recently have a few authors investigated the potential gains of international diversification.

A Segmentation Approach

Modern capital theory has strongly stimulated the study of the American capital market, while empirical tests of stock prices behavior on other markets have been very limited.

Since most of the work on the New York Stock Exchange is well known, it is not going to be summarized here. For the earlier tests of the random walk hypothesis, one might consult Cootner [6] and Fama [10]. Sharpe [38] and Jensen [20] provide good summaries of the recent work on the market model and capital asset pricing model.

The number of publications applying modern capital theory to the study of other stock markets (especially European) is very limited. This is probably due to the lack of public and organized sources of stock price data. However, a few studies can be mentioned both on the random walk and market model.

Tests of the Random Walk. Several studies investigate whether European stock prices followed a random walk. One of the early and most basic contributions to the random walk theory originated in the U.K. by Kendall [21]. He studied industrial share indices on the London Stock Exchange for the period 1928-1938 and did not find any evidence of significant serial correlation. More recently, a group of English and Scottish economists have studied U.K. stock market indices. For instance Dryden [7] applied a simple Markov scheme to successive daily numbers of advances and declines on the London Stock Exchange. According to Dryden's results the random walk theory is violated on the London Stock Exchange. Thus, in his own words, the probability for a share to go up one day is seven times larger if it went up the previous day than if it went down (this implies substantial positive serial correlation).

Similarly Henri Theil [41] applies information theory to the daily percentage of stocks advancing, declining, or remaining at a constant price on the Amsterdam Stock Exchange from 1959 to 1963. Like Dryden, he finds results inconsistent with a random walk hypothesis and suggesting positive serial correlation: "The best prediction (information theory criterion) for tomorrow is half-way between a long run average and today's observation." Fama [11] replicated this test on the New York Stock Exchange but did not find that present changes could help to forecast future changes in prices. While these tests were based on market aggregates, Solnik [39] used individual stock prices of 268 securities from eight European countries; the random walk hypothesis has been tested on each European market and the results confronted with comparable evidence on the American market. The distributions of serial correlation coefficients do not look fully consistent with the random walk hypothesis; in that respect the European markets seem slightly less efficient than the New York Stock Exchange. Surprisingly, individual serial correlation coefficients seem to be rather predictable on all markets: A stock displaying a price pattern with positive (or negative) serial correlation in one period will keep this characteristic in the following periods.[a]

Tests of the Market Model and CAPM. As far as tests of the market model or capital asset pricing model are concerned, little work has been done on the European markets. Solnik [39] computed the domestic systematic risk of 268 European securities. The R-square coefficients of the regressions of the stocks return versus the market return are of the order to magnitude of their American equivalent. The stability over time of the betas and of various statistics for individual stock has also been investigated with similar results.

---

[a]The cross-sectional correlation between estimates of the two periods is, for example, equal to the 0.48 for daily serial correlation coefficients of French stocks and 0.27 for biweekly coefficients. However, no European market seems to exhibit, on the whole, any systematic positive or negative time dependence.

Modigliani, Pogue, Scholes, and Solnik [30] tested the capital asset pricing model for the major European markets. When portfolios are used to estimate the relation between risk and return, the CAPM seems to be good description of the pricing mechanism. However this is not the case for Germany, where the systematic risk for individual stocks or portfolios is very unstable.

The International Approach

Grubel [15], Levy and Sarnat [24], and Grubel and Fadner [16] have presented studies on multinational equity markets using the same approach. Grubel, for example, is concerned with the range of potential gains to U.S. investors from international diversification. He postulates potential gains from international diversification by looking at the low correlation between national indices. The indices used in those studies are often not representative and do not integrate dividends; those tests also suffer from the small sample bias, since few observations are generally used. These correlation tests have been replicated on our data using different time intervals. In all cases, the correlation coefficients are extremely low (the R-square is seldom larger than 0.10). These tests and other published results are presented in Tables 5-1 to 5-6. Looking at the correlation coefficients computed on our data, it appears that the coefficients increase with the time interval used, but not dramatically (as long as the number of observations is sufficient and the small sample bias not too important). The mean weekly serial correlation coefficient is equal to 0.172. For biweekly returns, the average coefficient is 0.212, and 0.278 for monthly returns.

Although these intercountry correlations are generally significantly different from zero,[b] they are very small and indicate potential reductions in risk through international diversification.

The correlations with the U.S. index found by various authors are included in Table 5-6. While not in perfect agreement, these different numbers are not

---

[b]If the returns have finite variance, and in a large sample of time observations, the standard deviation of the serial correlation coefficient is approximated by the Anderson formula:

$$SD = \frac{1}{\sqrt{N}}$$

SD(week) = 0.061 SD(2 weeks) = 0.087 SD(month = 0.124)

Most of the coefficients presented in Tables 5-1, 5-2, and 5-3 are larger than one standard deviation from zero.

Table 5-1
Intercountry Correlation Weekly Returns, March 1966–April 1971

	U.S.A.	U.K.	France	Japan	Germany	Italy	Neth.	Belgium	Swed.	Swiss.
U.S.A.	1.00	.236	.154	.124	.236	.133	.420	.240	.118	.366
U.K.		1.00	.077	.293	.116	.131	.268	.124	.051	.136
France			1.00	.125	.183	.195	.158	.193	.251	.139
Japan				1.00	.124	.035	.171	.058	.116	.081
Germany					1.00	.156	.268	.263	.140	.261
Italy						1.00	.206	.076	.049	.198
Netherlands							1.00	.149	.154	.357
Belgium								1.00	.157	.269
Sweden									1.00	.066
Switzerland										1.00

Table 5-2
Intercountry Correlation Biweekly Returns, March 1966–April 1971

	U.S.A.	U.K.	France	Japan	Germany	Italy	Neth.	Belgium	Swed.	Swiss.
U.S.A.	1.00	.203	.050	.181	.232	.102	.503	.302	.148	.359
U.K.		1.00	.121	.299	.162	.039	.248	.140	.098	.148
France			1.00	.112	.283	.277	.140	.222	.244	.183
Japan				1.00	.176	.172	.271	.037	.201	.218
Germany					1.00	.192	.405	.305	.260	.362
Italy						1.00	.204	.130	.211	.203
Netherlands							1.00	.166	.211	.461
Belgium								1.00	.214	.272
Sweden									1.00	.168
Switzerland										1.00

Table 5-3
Intercountry Correlation Monthly Returns, March 1966–April 1971

	U.S.A.	U.K.	France	Japan	Germany	Italy	Neth.	Belgium	Swed.	Swiss.
U.S.A.	1.00	.202	.056	.194	.224	.068	.508	.475	.291	.445
U.K.		1.00	.113	.321	.192	.191	.284	.173	.207	.186
France			1.00	.107	.283	.330	.168	.382	.185	.320
Japan				1.00	.236	.224	.264	.172	.198	.211
Germany					1.00	.219	.474	.458	.321	.535
Italy						1.00	.248	.160	.225	.324
Netherlands							1.00	.410	.335	.525
Belgium								1.00	.320	.514
Sweden									1.00	.238
Switzerland										1.00

Table 5-4
Correlation Coefficients After Grubel and Fadner, 1965-1967

	Weekly			Monthly		
	U.S.A.	U.K.	Germany	U.S.A.	U.K.	Germany
U.S.A.	1.00	.09	.06	1.00	.21	.05
U.K.		1.00	.02		1.00	.11
Germany			1.00			1.00

Table 5-5
Correlation Coefficients After Agmon (Monthly), 1961-1965

	U.S.A.	U.K.	Germany	Japan
U.S.A.	1.00	.350	.392	.200
U.K.		1.00	.278	.130
Germany			1.00	.139
Japan				1.00

inconsistent and indicate some stability over time since different periods were used by the various authors.

Grubel, Levy, and Sarnat have also computed the expost international efficient set[1] in a mean variance framework; all national portfolios are dominated by international investment. This efficient set has been computed on our sample and appears in Figure 5-1. However, it is impossible to draw any strong conclusion on one expost observation of the efficient set.[2] Besides, the period is relatively short (5 years) and differences in taxes, etc., are hard to capture.

More recently, Agmon [1], tried to apply capital-asset-pricing-model types of tests to stock prices of some Japanese, American, British and German securities. Since his tests are not based on a theoretical model they are hard to interpret. The quality of the data (capital adjustments not included) and the estimation procedure[3] cast doubt on the validity of the results.

Table 5-6
Correlation with the U.S.

U.K.	Germany	Japan	Italy	France	Netherlands	Belgium	
.20	.22	.19	.07	.16	.51	.48	Solnik (Monthly) 1966–1971
.35	.39	.20	N.A.	N.A.	N.A.	N.A.	Agmon (Monthly) 1961–1965
.26	.43	N.A.	.09	.34	.53	.83	Levy, Sarnat (Yearly) 1951–1967
.21	.05	N.A.	N.A.	N.A.	N.A.	N.A.	Grubel and Fadner (Monthly) 1965–1967

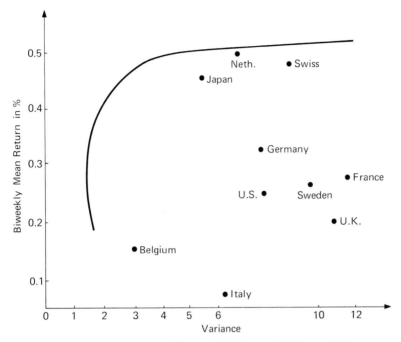

NB: Quadratic Programming System (QPS) was used. It is a modification of the program RS QPF4 written by Leola Cutler of the Rand Corporation. This program is supported by the Sloan School of Management.

Figure 5-1. Efficient Set of Country Indices.

Notes

1. An efficient portfolio is defined as a portfolio which maximizes expected return for a given standard deviation of the portfolio return, and minimizes standard deviation for a given expected return. The concept was originally introduced by Markowitz [27].

2. It would have been interesting to see how efficient portfolios build on the basis of these results behave in the following period. The relative stability of correlation coefficients indicate that this approach might be successful. However, five years of data were not sufficient for such a test.

3. Using individual securities to estimate cross-sectionally the market line leads to systematic bias due to errors-in-the-variable, as pointed out by Black, Jensen, and Scholes [3].

6 The Data

Data for Individual Countries

The data base used consisted of *daily* price and dividend data for 234 common stocks of eight major European countries. The data covered the period from March 1966 through April 1971.[1] The data were corrected for all capital adjustments (splits, rights, etc.); this feature can be very important since firms pay most of their earnings this way in some countries. In order to complete this data base a comparable sample of 65 American stocks has been included.[2]

The distribution of the sample by country is shown in Table 6-1. Within each country the companies in our sample tend to be the largest in terms of market value of shares outstanding. The 30 Italian stocks, for example, comprise 77 percent of the market value of all listed shares. For the United Kingdom, France, and Germany the number is not as high but is still in excess of 50 percent in each case. (Company names are given in Appendix B.)

Security returns were computed on a biweekly basis, as follows:[3]

$$r_t = \frac{P_t + d_t - P_{t-1}}{P_{t-1}}$$

where

r_t = the return during calendar interval t

P_t = stock price at the end of the two-week period

P_{t-1} = stock price at the end of the previous two-week period

d_t = dividends paid during the two-week period (assuming payments on ex-dividend dates)[a]

For each country the rates of return on a market index were computed on a comparable basis in particular the return on the index includes dividends for all countries. The indices chosen are described in Table 6-2. They are either the only

---

[a]Dividend data were not available for the Netherlands, Sweden and Switzerland; thus return is measured by the proportionate change in stock price.

Table 6-1
Summary of Data Base Used

Country	Number of Stocks in Sample	Market Index Used	Risk Free Rate Used
France	65	INSEE	Short term prime bank
Italy	30	24 ORE	Short term prime bank
United Kingdom	40	Financial Times, Industrial Ordinary	31 day treasury notes
Germany	35	Herstatt Index	Short term prime bank
Netherlands	24	ANP/CBS	Short term prime bank
Switzerland	17	Schweizerische Kreditanstalt	Short term prime bank
Belgium	17	Indice de la Bourse de Bruxelles	Short term prime bank
Sweden	6	Jacobson & Ponsbach	Short term prime bank
United States	65	Standard & Poor's 500 Stock Composite Index	30 day U.S. Government Treasury Bills
Japan		All Shares, 1st Section	Short term prime bank

Table 6-2
Composition of the National Indices

Country	Index	How many securities and what rules of section?	What weighting system is used?	Method of averaging	How frequently is the index published?	Is the price adjusted for accrued interest or dividend?
France	INSEE	50 Selected in accordance with the volume of deals	Overall index is weighted average of group indices, weights being proportionate to market value capitalization. Subindices are not weighted.	Arithmetic	Daily	Yes (but not in the original index)
Italy	24 ORE	N.A. (large number)	Weighted by share capital	Arithmetic	Daily	"
U.K.	Financial Times	30 Firms operating mostly in Britain in manufacturing or distribution	Not weighted	Geometric	Daily	"
Germany	Herstatt	100 All classes	Weighted by share capital	Arithmetic	Daily	"
Neth.	ANP/CBS	53 Selection made in consultation with various experts	Group indices not weighted. Overall index is the weighted average of group indices, the weights being share turnover in the base period (1953)	Arithmetic	Daily	"
Swiss	Schweizerische Kreditanstalt	25 shares quoted on Zurich	Not weighted	Arithmetic	Daily	"
Belgium	Indice de la Bourse de Bruxelles	All listed securities	Not weighted	Arithmetic	Daily	"
Sweden	Jacobson and Ponsbach	N.A.	N.A.	N.A.	Daily	"
U.S.A.	Standard & Poor 500	500	Weighted by share market value relative to updated base value	Arithmetic	Daily	"
Japan	All shares of 1st section	225	Not weighted	Arithmetic	Daily	"

Table 6-3
Estimated Market Value of All Shares Outstanding in 1966
(in billions dollars)

	Bond	Common Stock	Total	GNP (in 1970)
France	15	20.8	35.8	164
Italy	17	20.3	37.3	99
U.K.	57	161.3	228	141
Germany	21	18	49	213
Switzerland	3.4	5.9	9.3	23
Netherlands	6	3.5	9.5	36
Belgium	5	5	10	26
Sweden	7	3	10	39
Japan	18.5	22.2	40.7	237
U.S.A.	130	515	645	974

Note: This includes the market value of all the securities listed on all the capital markets of each country (excluding government bonds not listed on the general stock exchange), with the exceptions of:

    U.K.:   Only London Stock Exchange
    France: Only Bourse de Paris
    U.S.A.: On the New York Stock Exchange only

Sources:

France:	Chambre syndicale des Agents de Change
Italy:	Banca D'Italia
U.K.:	London Stock Exchange, Annual Report
Germany:	Wirtschaft und Statistik
Switzerland:	OECD, Committee on Invisible Transactions
Netherlands:	Maandstaatistiek van het Financiewezen
Belgium:	Commission de la Bourse de Bruxelles
Sweden:	Sveriges Riksbank, Arsbok
Japan:	Bank of Japan
U.S.A.:	Survey of Current Business

indices available or, where choice existed, the most representative. An index for the Japanese market has also been constructed.

Finally, interest rates on some risk free comparable securities have been collected for the ten countries. The rates chosen appear in Table 6-1. These statistics have been compiled from the International Monetary Fund Monthly Statistics [18] and the EEC Monthly Statistics [9].

Data for International Comparisons

Comparing statistics from different countries is a difficult task. The results will be only as good as the accuracy of the data collected on each country. This is the reason why national indices have been carefully selected and include dividends. These returns were compared with indices built from the sample of stocks used in this study. In all cases the correlations were very high (over .90). Since the official indices are more broadly based, they will be used for international comparisons.

An international index was built from these indices. The theory claims for an index with market value weights. Since the market weight for each stock should have been computed, we are faced with the same technical problem as in the American case. Besides the total country capitalization as given in Table 6-3 is not representative of the total amount of investment opportunities of a given country (it is markedly too large for the U.K. and too small for Japan and Germany). Among the variables more representative of *total* investment opportunities in a country, the Gross National Product seemed to be the best choice. Therefore, the international index was built using GNP weights. For each country, the returns are computed in the local currency as required by the international asset pricing model.

Notes

1. I wish to thank Eurofinance for making their stock price tape available to me. Without this data the present study would have been impossible.
2. To have a sample of U.S. stocks comparable in size and quality with the European data, 65 securities were randomly selected from the ISL daily prices tape, 15 of those stocks were constrained to be among the 60 largest firms on the exchange. I wish to thank Professor Myron Scholes for his help in collecting these data.
3. The theoretical model suggests the use of small time intervals, possibly days. However the measurement errors (bad data, . . .) involved in the use of daily returns are large and strongly affect the results. The biweekly interval was chosen (as opposed to daily or monthly intervals) as a compromise between the problems of measurement error inherent in daily data and sampling inefficiencies associated with longer intervals. A discussion of the effects on the CAPM parameters of changes in the return measurement interval is contained in Solnik [39].

7

Test of the Single Market Model

An International "Single Index Model"

In Part I a theoretical model of international relation between capital markets has been presented; it will now be tested in its simple form.

Under the assumptions given in Part I it has been possible to establish a relation between the expected return and the international risk of a security:

$$\alpha_i - R_i = \beta_i(\alpha_m - R_m) \tag{30}$$

where

α_i is the expected return on security i (in local currency)

R_i is the interest rate in the country of security i (in local currency)

α_m is the expected return on the world market portfolio (where each component is expressed in its own currency)

R_m is the average interest rate in the world

$\beta_i = \dfrac{\sigma_{im}}{\sigma_m^2}$ is the international systematic risk of security i

In other words, the excess expected return of a security (over the risk free rate of its country) is equal to a risk premium given by the product of the systematic international risk by the world market risk premium.

Equation (30) is stated in terms of the expected returns on any security or portfolio i and the expected returns on the market portfolio. Since these expectations are strictly unobservable, we wish to show how (30) can be recast in terms of the objectively measurable realizations of returns on any portfolio i and the market M. The same problem is present for the test of a single market asset pricing model and a special structure of asset returns has to be postulated. For individual countries it was generally assumed a particular relation between security returns called the "market model."[1] In this chapter it will be assumed that all securities returns are affected by only one common factor, the "market factor" of a single world market.

$$\tilde{r}_i = \alpha_i + \beta_i(\tilde{r}_m - E(\tilde{r}_m)) + \tilde{\epsilon}_i \tag{31}$$

where

$\tilde{r}_i$ is the (realized) return on security i

α_i is the expected return on security i

$\tilde{r}_m$ is the (realized) return on the "market factor" which, to a close approximation, is equal to the return on the world market portfolio[2]

$E(\tilde{r}_m)$ is the expected return on the "market factor":

$$E(\tilde{r}_m) \sim \alpha_m$$

The variables $\tilde{\epsilon}_i$ and $\tilde{\pi} = \tilde{r}_m - E(\tilde{r}_m)$ are assumed to be normal random variables with:

$$E(\tilde{\epsilon}_i) = 0 \qquad \text{for all } i$$

$$\text{Cov}(\tilde{\epsilon}_i, \tilde{\pi}) = 0$$

$$\text{Cov}(\tilde{\epsilon}_i, \tilde{\epsilon}_j) = \begin{cases} 0 & \text{if } i \neq j \\ \sigma^2 & \text{if } i = j \end{cases}$$

Thus, assuming that the international asset pricing model is valid, (31) can be substituted in (30)

$$\tilde{r}_i - \beta_i(\tilde{r}_m - \alpha_m) - \epsilon_i - R_i = \beta_i(\alpha_m - R_m)$$

therefore

$$\tilde{r}_i - R_i = \beta_i(\tilde{r}_m - R_m) + \epsilon_i \tag{32}$$

This says that the excess realized returns on any security or portfolio can be expressed as a linear function of its systematic risk.

Equation (32) can be easily subjected to empirical testing through cross-sectional regression, once the international systematic risk of securities has been computed. Most of the least square necessary conditions are satisfied *if* the market model is a good description of the security returns relations, since:

$$\epsilon_i \sim N(0, \sigma^2)$$

$$\text{Cov}(\epsilon_i, \epsilon_j) = \begin{cases} 0 & \text{if } i \neq j \\ \sigma^2 & \text{if } i = j \end{cases}$$

In the following sections the international risk of individual securities and portfolios will be computed and equation (32) will be tested cross-sectionally. It is important to use average realized *excess* returns since different risks free rate R_i are used. In the single market CAPM this was not so important, since the same risk free rate appeared on both sides of the expression.

Estimations of the International Risk

All indices and securities returns have been regressed on the world index returns. This means that biweekly time series have been used to estimate the following equation:

$$r_{it} = \alpha_i + \beta_i r_{mt} + \epsilon_{it}$$

The results for national indices, which can be considered as approximations of the country market portfolios, are given in Table 7–1.

Switzerland and the Netherlands seem to have high betas relative to the world index. Besides, the percentage of variation explained by the world factor is high in both cases (0.53 and 0.44). This was to be expected since the Dutch and Swiss markets are the most internationally oriented, with no restriction of foreign investment.

The international systematic risk of individual stocks has been computed; the average beta for those stocks is equal to 1.08 with a sample dispersion (standard deviation) of 0.39. The percentage of price variance attributable to the international factor is generally not very high, as could be expected; the average R-square for the period is 14 percent. For the period March 1967–April 1971 the mean return has been 0.41 percent biweekly. The sample dispersion (standard deviation) of those mean returns is equal to 0.40; this figure indicates great differences in return among stocks.

In these time series regressions it would have been better to use risk premiums instead of returns to estimate the international systematic risk of security and national indices. However the lack of weekly interest rates for all countries made this task impossible. Although dropping the interest rate could introduce a systematic bias in time series estimates of betas, these estimations should not be affected very much because of (at least) two reasons:

Table 7–1

Time Series Regressions of National Indices vs. World Index,
March 1967–April 1971

	$r_i = \alpha_i + \beta_i r_m + \epsilon_i$			Standard deviation of returns in % (biweekly)	Mean return in % (biweekly)	Average risk free rate in % (biweekly)
	α (stand. dev.)	β (stand. dev.)	R^2			
World				1.47	0.440	0.210
U.S.A.	−0.17 (0.20)	0.98 (0.13)	0.34	2.49	0.255	0.220
U.K.	−0.24 (0.30)	1.17 (0.20)	0.25	3.42	0.268	0.295
France	0.06 (0.30)	1.11 (0.18)	0.26	3.20	0.544	0.235
Japan	0.21 (0.22)	0.88 (0.14)	0.28	2.43	0.593	0.239
Germany	0.01 (0.20)	1.10 (0.14)	0.38	2.63	0.494	0.190
Italy	−0.17 (0.25)	0.88 (0.15)	0.25	2.56	0.214	0.165
Netherlands	0.00 (0.20)	1.22 (0.11)	0.52	2.49	0.533	0.200
Belgium	0.14 (0.17)	0.43 (0.10)	0.14	1.67	0.330	0.208
Sweden	0.00 (0.22)	0.92 (0.17)	0.23	2.84	0.403	0.240
Switzerland	0.15 (0.19)	1.30 (0.15)	0.44	2.91	0.715	0.136

A typical biweekly stock return is 4 or 5%, while a maximum deviation from the mean for an interest rate would be of the order of 2 or 3% *annually* (a *biweekly* rate of 0.1%). Therefore the effect is very small. This is even true for indices where a mean biweekly change is 2.5%.

While the interest rates would have relatively no importance when using short time intervals, this argument would not be true any more if one was testing time series of annual observations. Besides interest rates should be (and are) considered for cross-sectional tests of the model.

If the variations in interest rates are orthogonal to the market risk, then it will not make any difference whether returns or risk premiums are used. This independence has generally been assumed in the U.S. tests of the capital asset pricing model. The same type of assumption is implicit here. Some empirical evidence on the U.S. market shows that the betas are very robust. Using both returns and risk premiums, Conway [5] computed the betas of 117 mutual funds for a 10-year period (monthly observations). Since mutual funds hold diversified portfolios the change in returns is smaller than for individual stocks. Besides, the interval used is a month and one would expect a larger effect due to the interest rate since its variations are relatively larger.

However he finds very little difference, if any, between risk estimates computed from returns or risk premiums. Running a cross-sectional regression between betas estimated on risk premium, and returns he gets the following results:

$$\hat{\beta}(\text{returns}) = -0.002 \quad + 1.002 \quad \times \ \beta(\text{risk premium})$$
$$\phantom{\hat{\beta}(\text{returns}) = } (.0004) \quad (.0004)$$

$$R^2 = 0.999$$

There is no reason to believe that the same kind of results would not be found in the international case.

Security Cross-Sectional Results

Once the systematic risk has been computed, a cross-sectional regression was run to test the relationship between mean return and risk. As outlined above, the following relation was tested:

$$\bar{\rho}_i = \bar{r}_i - \bar{R}_i = a_0 + a_1 \hat{\beta}_i + \epsilon_i \tag{33}$$

where

$\bar{r}_i$ is the average return on the security or portfolio, generally for the period March 1967–April 1971.

$\bar{R}_i$ is the average risk free rate for the country where security i is listed, during the same period. These values are given in Table 7-1.

$\bar{\rho}_i$ is the risk premium or excess return for that security or portfolio.

$\hat{\beta}_i$ is the estimated international risk (from the time series regression).

and the estimated coefficients $\hat{a}_0$ and $\hat{a}_1$ were compared with their theoretical values 0 and $\bar{r}_m - \bar{R}_m$ as given by the IAPM.

A first idea of the validity of the international pricing of risk can be

obtained by running this regression on national indices. The relation between
mean excess return and risk is given by:

$$\bar{\rho}_i = -0.08 + 0.31 \ \hat{\beta}_i$$
$$\quad\quad (0.20) \quad (0.20)$$

$$R^2 = 0.21$$

Higher risk country indices had higher rates of return as predicted by the
IAPM, with return increasing 0.31 percent per two weeks (8.3 percent per year)
for a one unit increase in β. While the sign of a_1 is in agreement with the IAPM
predictions, it is larger than the 0.21 percent predicted value (see Table 7-2) and
the intercept term is negative instead of being equal to zero. However these
results are very gratifying since the coefficients are of the magnitude predicted
and do not disprove statistically the international asset pricing model. Besides
the percentage of cross-section mean return accounted for by the risk coefficient
is relatively large, 21 percent.

Let us now estimate the coefficients a_0 and a_1 using individual securities.
The estimated relation between excess return and risk is:

$$\bar{\rho}_i = 0.14 + 0.08 \ \hat{\beta}_i$$
$$\quad\quad (0.08) \quad (0.07)$$

$$R^2 = 0.01$$

Although there seems to exist a positive relation between international risk
and returns, the estimated coefficients differ significantly from their predicted
values. Besides, the proportion of cross-section mean return accounted for by
the risk coefficients is very low.

One should not draw hasty conclusions from the result of this security
regression. In their tests of the capital asset pricing model on the American market, Black, Jensen, and Scholes [3] have presented evidence that individual
securities should not be used to test that kind of relation, because of an errors-
in-the-variables bias. A testing design will now be developed to correct for this
bias.

Portfolio Grouping of Securities

If the assumptions of the least squares regression procedure were met, then
the estimates of a_0 and a_1 obtained from the security regressions would be the

Table 7–2
Test of the IAMP Assuming a Single Index Model

	$(\bar{r}_i - R_i = \hat{a}_0 + \hat{a}_1\beta_i)$			Number of indices or portfolios
	$\hat{a}_0$ (stand. dev.)	$\hat{a}_1$ (stand. dev.)	R^2	
Theoretical Values	0	0.23		
Indices	-0.08 (0.20)[a]	0.31 (0.20)	0.21	10
Individual securities	0.14 (0.08)	0.08 (0.07)	0.01	299
All national portfolios	0.04 (0.11)	0.19 (0.10)	0.06	73
International portfolios	-0.07 (0.04)	0.26 (0.04)	0.86	8
U.S. portfolios	-0.16 (0.10)	0.12 (0.08)	0.11	18
French portfolios	0.04 (0.10)	0.29 (0.10)	0.35	17
U.K. portfolios	-0.07 (0.13)	0.18 (0.10)	0.25	12
German portfolios	-1.11 (1.35)	1.32 (1.21)	0.13	10
Italian portfolios	-0.21 (0.20)	0.21 (0.20)	0.12	10
Belgian portfolios	-0.10	1.40		2
Dutch portfolios	0.14	0.14		2
Swiss portfolios	-1.64	1.5		2

[a]Standard deviation.

most efficient possible. However, this is not the case, since the independent variable in the cross-section regressions, β_j, is measured with error. As long as $\hat{\beta}_j$ contains measurement error, the estimates of $\hat{a}_0$ and $\hat{a}_1$ will be subject to the well known errors-in-the-variable bias and will be inconsistent. The result of this bias is that $\hat{a}_1$ will be understated and $\hat{a}_0$ correspondingly overstated. Hence tests of relationship between $\hat{a}_0$ and $\hat{a}_1$ and their theoretical values 0, $\bar{r}_m - \bar{R}_m$ will be misleading.

There are a variety of methods available to attempt to correct for this bias.[3] One particularly effective method involves classifying the observations into groups (portfolios) and fitting the group means. To obtain consistent estimates from the grouping process two conditions are required: First, the securities must be classified into portfolios independently of the values of the errors in the $\hat{\beta}_j$ estimates, since otherwise the law of large numbers would not apply to reduce the error in the portfolio β. Second, the beta values of the different portfolios (the averages of the component securities) should differ as much as possible if good estimates of a_0 and a_1 are to be obtained.

These requirements are jointly fulfilled in the following way. The securities were ranked by their estimated beta values relative to their *country* index in the period March 1966–February 1967. National portfolios were then formed grouping the securities into portfolios.

National Portfolios

The first (national) portfolio contained the first subgroup of stock of this country with the highest (national) beta, and so on until all securities were included in portfolios. Mean returns and international beta coefficients were then estimated for each portfolio during the March 1967–April 1971 period. The previous cross-sectional regressions were then rerun by regressing the mean portfolio returns on the corresponding estimated portfolio betas to obtain revised estimates of a_0 and a_1. The initial period ranking procedure tends to eliminate the correlation between the measurement errors on the second period betas of the securities classified into each portfolio, thus meeting the first grouping requirement. Besides, this instrumental variable turns out to provide a good spread in the international β's of portfolios because the correlation between national and international systematic risk is relatively large.

The advantage of this approach is that it yields unbiased (for large portfolios) and efficient (for many portfolios) estimates of a_0 and a_1. The tradeoff between these two properties becomes very important, particularly in our case where the number of securities in each European sample is small.

To obtain the major benefit of the law of large numbers to reduce measurement error, at least ten securities have been included in each portfolio. This, however, leaves a relatively small number of portfolios for each country. For example for France there are five portfolios of twelve stocks; for Italy, three portfolios of ten stocks. To increase the number of portfolios additional grouping schemes were used. One scheme was to construct "overlapping" portfolios where the same security would appear in more than one portfolio. For each country the stocks were ranked as before on their March 1966–February 1967 estimated national risk. The first portfolio was then made up of the fifteen securities with the highest estimated β values.

The second was composed of fifteen securities including some of the lowest risk stocks from the first portfolio plus additional securities ranked below the first fifteen. The amount of overlap depends on the sample size and the number of portfolios desired. A second alternative was to dichotomize the population into portfolios containing the highest and lowest β securities. The resulting number of portfolios[a] for each country appears in Table 7-2.

These national portfolios will be used to test the IAPM for each country and compare the results. In Chapter 8 a multinational model will be presented whose test requires such national diversified portfolios.

International Portfolios

Finally, some internationally diversified portfolios were built from this set of portfolios. Only nonoverlapping national portfolios were used; therefore any security appears only in one internationally diversified portfolio. The same kind of instrumental variable and grouping procedure was used. The international beta of country portfolios were estimated in the period March 1966–February 1967 and international portfolios (both European and worldwide) were built using that ranking. Mean returns and international betas were then estimated for the period March 1967–April 1971. A description of those international portfolios is given in Table 7-3.

In summary, the construction of these portfolios is a two-step procedure. There is first a diversification at the country level, then an international grouping of those portfolios bringing an international diversification. Another alternative is the direct grouping of all securities into portfolios according to their international systematic risk of the first period. The first method was chosen because of its greater convenience to take into account risk premiums and national factors and to compare national and international results. The computations performed with the second method yielded very similar cross-sectional regression results.

Portfolio Cross-Sectional Regression

Several regressions were run using those portfolio data to estimate the coefficients of:

---

[a]See Modigliani, Pogue, Scholes, and Solnik [30] for a more detailed description of these portfolios.

$$\bar{\rho}_i = a_0 + a_1 \hat{\beta}_i + \epsilon_i$$

These results are given in Table 7–2. When the mean return and beta of all the *national* portfolios are considered (73 portfolios) the results are consistent with the model. The estimated relation is:

$$\bar{\rho}_i = \underset{(0.11)}{0.04} + \underset{(0.10)}{0.19} \hat{\beta}_i$$

while the IAPM predicted $a_0 = 0$ and $a_1 = 0.23$. However the R^2 of this regression is very low (equal to 0.06), and the standard deviations quite large.

Table 7–3
Composition of the International Portfolios

	Number of stocks	Country	World beta	Mean return in % (biweekly)
Portfolio 1	31	Switzerland (8) U.K. (10) Netherlands (12) U.S.A. (11)	1.51	0.556
Portfolio 2	45	Netherlands (12) France (12) U.K. (10) U.S.A. (11)	1.37	0.551
Portfolio 3	30	U.K. (10) Switzerland (9) Germany (11)	1.15	0.450
Portfolio 4	33	U.K. (10) Germany (12) U.S.A. (11)	1.13	0.418
Portfolio 5	44	Italy (10) France (12) Germany (11) U.S.A. (11)	1.05	0.456
Portfolio 6	28	Sweden (6) Italy (10) France (12)	0.98	0.466
Portfolio 7	41	France (12) Italy (10) Belgium (8) U.S.A. (11)	0.85	0.393
Portfolio 8	31	Belgium (9) France (12) U.S.A. (10)	0.69	0.340

Table 7–4
Time Series Statistics of the International Portfolios
March 1967–April 1971
$(\tilde{r}_{it} = \alpha_i + \beta_i \tilde{r}_{mt} + \epsilon_{it})$

	α_i in % (biweekly returns)	β_i	R^2
Portfolio 1	-0.15 (0.22)[a]	1.51 (0.07)	0.78
Portfolio 2	0.08 (0.14)	1.37 (0.05)	0.89
Portfolio 3	0.26 (0.15)	1.15 (0.06)	0.72
Portfolio 4	-0.05 (0.37)	1.13 (0.07)	0.67
Portfolio 5	0.01 (0.12)	1.05 (0.06)	0.73
Portfolio 6	0.16 (0.19)	0.98 (0.10)	0.51
Portfolio 7	0.10 (0.16)	0.85 (0.05)	0.73
Portfolio 8	-0.14 (0.31)	0.69 (0.05)	0.62

[a]Standard deviation.

The results of the regression for the eight world diversified portfolios are even more in support of the international asset pricing model with:

$$\bar{\rho}_i = -0.07 + 0.26\ \beta_i$$
$$(0.04)\quad(0.04)$$

and

$$R^2 = 0.87$$

Although the slope is slightly larger than was forecast (0.23), its t-statistic is 6.2, indicating an excellent fit. This result strongly supports the international asset pricing model.

The same cross-sectional regression has also been run for the national portfolios of each of the major stock exchanges (U.K., France, Germany, and Italy). While the British and French securities exhibit the international pricing of risk

postulated by the IAPM, the same conclusions cannot be reached for Italy
(intercept of -0.21) and Germany.[4]

Securities for Switzerland, Belgium, and the Netherlands were grouped into
two portfolios per country, and the slope and intercept of the line joining those
portfolios were estimated. It is apparent that for all these countries there exists a
positive relation between mean realized returns and the international systematic
risk; however, the coefficient of this relation seems to vary for securities of different countries. This suggests a new and more realistic specification of the
security price structure, which would still be supported by the excellent empirical results for international diversified portfolios under this model specification.

Notes

1. Initially called the "diagonal model" it has been analyzed in considerable
    detail by Sharpe [35], [36], and empirically tested by Blume [4] in the
    U.S. market and Solnik [39] on the European markets. The somewhat
    more descriptive term "market model" was suggested by Fama [12].
2. Fama [12] pointed out that if one chooses to interpret the market factor
    as an average of security returns (market index) or as the return on the
    market portfolio M, the specifications of the market model will not hold.

    However, at a first approximation:

    $$\text{Cov}\,(\tilde{\epsilon}_i, \tilde{\pi}) \sim 0$$

    and

    $$\alpha_m = E(\tilde{r}_m)\,.$$

    Since the error of approximation is very slight, we will henceforth use the
    equality:

    $$\tilde{r}_i = \alpha_i + \beta_i(\tilde{r}_m - \alpha_m) + \tilde{\epsilon}_i\,.$$

3. See Malinvaud [26]. Black, Jensen, and Scholes [3] have applied these
    methods to NYSE data. Modigliani, Pogue, Scholes, and Solnik [30] have
    applied this procedure to European securities.
4. The betas of the German portfolios are very close (with large standard
    deviations). Thus one of the requirements of the grouping procedure has
    not been met, resulting in an inability to obtain estimates of a_0, a_1. The
    same characteristic was noticed in Solnik [39] and Modigliani, et al. [30]
    when studying the national pricing of risk: "The reason for the lack of

difference between the portfolio β results from a lack of stability in the beta coefficients for German stocks. Thus beta rankings in the March 1966–March 1967 period gave little information about betas during the next four years. Therefore, the β coefficients for the portfolios will differ only by chance."

8 A Multinational World Market

The single world index model which has been used to test the international asset pricing model relies on strong and specific assumptions. Especially, all security prices are supposed to be similarly affected by a single world factor, which is the sole common influence to all or part of these securities. The main criticism to the single index model is that all security prices of the same country tend to move together following domestic informations.

A Critique of the Single Index Model

The large degree of dependence on the country market behavior has been emphasized in earlier studies. King [23] and Blume [4] have shown the existence of a strong national market factor common to all U.S. securities. Testing an American index model on New York Stock Exchange securities, they found that the percentage of stock returns variance explained by the American market factor was generally high; on the average this proportion was of the order of 30 percent for the recent years. Similarly, Solnik [39] studied each European capital market separately. The strong dependence on national factors is evidenced by the results presented in Table 8-1. Also given in this table is the average proportion of the variance of securities returns attributable to the international market factor. These two sets of figures have been estimated independently. It is clear that the common dependence on a world factor cannot be the only reason for the apparent covariations of security prices in each country. In many cases the national influence more than doubles the international influence.

In the previous chapter the international market line of the IAPM was estimated using portfolio cross-sectional regressions. Its estimation for portfolios of different countries yielded significantly different slopes (see Table 7-2). This also would tend to suggest a poor specification of the model, not taking into account national characteristics.

A direct test of the single world index specification would be to look at the residuals of the world market model regressions. If our critique is founded, we would expect the residuals for various securities of the same country to be posi-

Table 8-1

Proportions of Security Risk Explained by National or International Factors (1966-1971, biweekly returns)

Country	Average proportion of variance attributable to national (market) variations (%)^a	Average proportion of variance attributable to international (market) variations (%)^b
France	30	9
Italy	46	14
U.K.	37	11
Germany	45	16
Netherlands	23	18
Belgium	16	15
Switzerland	35	21
Sweden	45	18
U.S.A.	22	16

^{a}R-square of the regression: $r_{k_i} = \alpha_{k_i} + \gamma_{k_i} I_k + \epsilon_{k_i}$ where I_k is the national index.

^{b}R-square of the regression: $r_{k_i} = \alpha_{k_i} + \beta_{k_i} I_m + \epsilon_{k_i}$ where I_m is the world index.

tively correlated while the model claims for uncorrelated error terms. As an illustration, the five independent portfolios made up of all the French securities included in the sample were considered. The pairwise correlation coefficients of their residuals are given in Table 8-2.

These correlation coefficients represent an R-square of 50 to 70 percent as opposed to 80 to 90 percent for portfolio returns. These figures are still very large and prove the existence of positive serial correlation between portfolio residuals of one country. Similarly the average pairwise correlation coefficient for individual French stocks is 0.47 ($R^2 = 0.22$).

All these results suggest that a multinational index model would provide a more realistic interpretation of international stock price behavior.

A "Nationalistic" Multi-Index Model

The Specification

A stochastic security price process that will respect the national characteristics of the international capital market structure would be more appropriate. The most "nationalistic" specification consistent with the IAPM postulates that on each market place, security prices have in common a national factor, which is

Table 8–2
Correlation Coefficients of French Portfolios Residuals

Portfolio	1	2	3	4	5
1		0.82	0.82	0.75	0.64
2			0.87	0.81	0.71
3				0.84	0.73
4					0.74
5					

in turn dependent on a single common world factor. In other words, all securities are affected by the international factor through their national index.

For a security k_i of country k, this can be written as:

$$\tilde{r}_{k_i} = \alpha_{k_i} + \gamma_{k_i}(\tilde{I}_k - E(\tilde{I}_k)) + \eta_{k_i} \qquad \text{for all } i \qquad (34)$$

where

$\tilde{r}_{k_i}$ is the (realized) return on security k_i of country k

$\tilde{I}_k$ is the (realized) return on the national index of country k

$E(\tilde{I}_k)$ is the expected return on that index, $E(\tilde{I}_k) = \alpha_k$

γ_{k_i} is the *national* systematic risk of security k_i

As in the previous chapter, the same approximation is made between the common factor and the index. Thus:

$$\tilde{I}_k = \alpha_k + \beta_k(\tilde{r}_m - \alpha_m) + \epsilon_k \qquad \text{for all } k \qquad (35)$$

where

$\tilde{r}_m$ is the (realized) return on the world market factor

α_m is its expected value

β_k is the international systematic risk of country k

The variables η_{k_i} and ϵ_k are assumed to be normal random variables with:

$$E(\eta_{k_i}) = E(\epsilon_k) = 0 \qquad \text{for all } k \text{ and } i$$

$$\text{cov}(\epsilon_k, \epsilon_{k'}) = \begin{cases} 0 & \text{if } k \neq k' \\ \sigma^2 & \text{if } k = k' \end{cases}$$

$$\text{cov}(\epsilon_k, \tilde{r}_m) = 0 \qquad \text{for all } k$$

$$\text{cov}(\epsilon_k, \eta_{k'_i}) = 0 \qquad \text{for all } k' \text{ and } k$$

$$\text{cov}(\eta_{k_i}, \eta_{k'_j}) = \begin{cases} 0 & \text{if } i \neq j \text{ or } k \neq k' \\ \sigma_i^2 & \text{if } i = j \text{ and } k = k' \end{cases} \qquad (36)$$

therefore

$$\text{cov}(\eta_{k_i}, \tilde{I}_k) = 0 \qquad \text{for all } i$$

$$\text{cov}(\eta_{k_i}, \tilde{r}_m) = 0 \qquad \text{for all } k \text{ and } i$$

A Testable Hypothesis

Before using this specification to test the IAPM, let us demonstrate an important result. If β_{k_i} is the international systematic risk of security k_i, it can be shown that this stochastic price process implies that β_{k_i} is equal to the product of the national systematic risk of that security, γ_{k_i}, by the international risk of its country, β_k:

$$\beta_{k_i} = \gamma_{k_i} \beta_k \qquad (37)$$

This can be shown by computing β_{k_i}

$$\beta_{k_i} = \frac{\text{cov}(\tilde{r}_{k_i}, \tilde{r}_m)}{\text{var}(\tilde{r}_m)}$$

from (34) and (35):

$$\beta_{i_k} = \frac{\text{cov}(\tilde{r}_m - \alpha_m, \gamma_{k_i}\beta_k(\tilde{r}_m - \alpha_m) + \gamma_{k_i}\epsilon_i + \eta_{k_i})}{\text{var}(\tilde{r}_m)}$$

But by construction we know that:

$$\text{cov}\,(\tilde{r}_m - \alpha_m,\, \epsilon_k) = 0$$

and

$$\text{cov}\,(\tilde{r}_m - \alpha_m,\, \eta_{k_i}) = 0$$

Therefore:

$$\beta_{k_i} = \gamma_{k_i}\beta_k \,\frac{\text{cov}\,(\tilde{r}_m - \alpha_m,\, \tilde{r}_m - \alpha_m)}{\text{var}\,(\tilde{r}_m)} = \gamma_{k_i}\beta_k$$

This is only true because all securities are only and identically affected by international variations through the national index since:

$$\text{cov}\,(\tilde{r}_m - \alpha_m,\, \eta_{k_i}) = 0$$

We now wish to show that the international pricing relation

$$\alpha_{k_i} - R_k = \beta_{k_i}\,(\alpha_m - R_m) \tag{30}$$

can be recast in terms of objectively measurable realizations of returns.

Being a linear relationship, equation (30) also applies to any portfolio of country k. In particular for the country market portfolio I_k:

$$\alpha_k - R_k = \beta_k(\alpha_m - R_m) \tag{38}$$

α_k and α_m can be substituted from (35) into (38) to get:

$$\bar{I}_k - R_k = \beta_k(\bar{r}_m - R_m) + \epsilon_k \tag{39}$$

This relation is the same as (32), established in the single index model framework, except that it only applies to national indices (or perfectly diversified national portfolios).

Substituting the value of $\bar{I}_i$ from (35) into (34), we get:

$$\tilde{r}_{k_i} - \alpha_{k_i} = \gamma_{k_i}\beta_k(\bar{r}_m - \alpha_m) + \gamma_{k_i}\epsilon_k + \eta_{k_i} \tag{40}$$

Since $\beta_{k_i} = \gamma_{k_i}\beta_k$, we can combine equation (40) and the IAPM (30), to eliminate expectation terms α_{k_i} and α_m:

$$\bar{r}_{k_i} - R_k = \beta_{k_i}(\bar{r}_m - R_m) + \gamma_{k_i}\epsilon_k + \eta_{k_i} = \gamma_{k_i}(\beta_k(\bar{r}_m - R_m) + \epsilon_k) + \eta_{k_i}$$

and from (39):

$$\bar{r}_{k_i} - R_k = \gamma_{k_i}(\bar{I}_k - R_k) + \eta_{k_i} \tag{41}$$

with cov $(\eta_{k_i}, \bar{I}_k - R_k) = 0$

The relation given in (41) is very interesting since it is identical to the testable relation of the national CAPM for a given country—assuming a market model. In fact, since this specification implies that the international systematic risk of a security is equal to its national systematic risk multiplied by the international risk of the country market, it can be shown that the pricing relation of the CAPM would hold for each country. The IAPM implies that:

$$\alpha_{k_i} - R_k = \beta_{k_i}(\alpha_m - R_m) \qquad \text{for all } k, i$$

and

$$\alpha_k - R_k = \beta_k(\alpha_m - R_m) \qquad \text{for all } k$$

since

$$\beta_{k_i} = \gamma_{k_i}\beta_k$$
$$\alpha_{k_i} - R_k = \gamma_{k_i}\beta_k(\alpha_m - R_m) = \gamma_{k_i}(\alpha_k - R_k) \quad \text{for all } i$$

Therefore the capital asset pricing model can be derived from the IAPM under this specification. This is a very important result since it makes the international model compatible with the results found for each national market separately. A test of the IAPM would simply be a test of the CAPM for the various national markets coupled with a test of the international relation (30) for national indices. This last relation is the only difference between an international market structure as postulated here and a segmented market structure with no international relations between perfect national capital markets.

Interesting implications can be derived from the consistency of the CAPM with the IAPM. The risk return pricing relation of, let us say, French stocks will be linear whether the sytematic risk on the French market or on the world market is considered. The slopes will only differ by a multiplicative factor. An investor unaware of international investment opportunities will still base his decisions on sound measures of relative risk since the excess return he can expect should be proportional to the national systematic risk or γ. However, even if he gets a perfect diversification on his (national) investment he is still left with some unique country risk which he could have diversified away internationally.

Test of the IAPM

Tests of the capital asset pricing model for the major European stock markets has been performed in Modigliani, Pogue, Scholes, and Solnik [30]. They also summarize the most careful studies on the American market. Table 8-3 gives the results of portfolio cross sectional regressions of equation (41), conducted independently for each country. Except in the case of Germany, these results provide some support to the capital asset pricing model for each country and therefore to the international asset pricing model. Other empirical research of the national risk-return relation on United States data has so far had mixed results.[1] The most careful examination performed by Black, Jensen, and Scholes shows that the relation between realized return and gamma appears to be linear as predicted by the CAPM. However the relation is not as strong as the theory suggests and riskier securities (large γ) earned less than predicted.

The results of the international regression for country indices support an international pricing of risk as it can be seen in Table 8-3:

$$\bar{I}_i - \bar{R}_i = -0.08 + 0.31\,\hat{\beta}_k$$
$$\qquad\quad (0.20)\quad (0.20) \qquad R^2 = 0.21$$

The estimated values of the coefficients are close to the values predicted by the IAPM: $a_0 = 0$, $a_1 = 0.23$. This would show that capital markets across the world are not segmented.

Conclusions

The results presented in this section, although consistent with the theory, can hardly be considered as irrefutable evidence in favor of the capital asset

Table 8-3

Test of the CAPM[a] (from Modigliani, et al., Table 3)

$$\bar{r}_i = a_0 + a_1 \hat{\gamma}_i + \eta_i$$

Country	No. of Portfolios	$\hat{a}_0$	$\hat{a}_1$	R^2	Theoretical Values	
					$a_0 = \bar{R}_k$	$a_1 = \bar{I}_k - \bar{R}_k$
France	17	0.19 (0.13)	0.30 (0.14)	0.33	0.33	0.30
Italy	9	0.38 (0.13)	0.12 (0.08)	0.23	0.24	0.25
U.K.	12	0.13 (0.09)	0.16 (0.09)	0.23	0.20	0.13
Germany	10	3.25 (0.55)	-2.54 (0.52)	0.74	0.36	0.21
U.S.A.	10	0.41 (0.31)	-0.22 (0.20)	0.55	0.48	-0.23

[a]For the period March 1967–April 1971 except for Italy and the U.S.A.: March 1967–June 1970.

Test of the IAPM, Regression of Indices

$$\bar{I}_k - \bar{R}_k = a_0 + a_1 \hat{\beta}_k + \epsilon_k$$

a_0	a_1	R^2	Theoretical Values	
			$a_0 = 0$	$a_1 = \bar{r}_m - \bar{R}_m$
-0.08 (0.20)	0.31 (0.20)	0.21	0	0.23

pricing model and therefore the international asset pricing model. One obvious criticism can be made to improve this multinational index specification. This "nationalistic" model postulates that all stock prices are identically affected by international price movements through their national index. This is a rather unrealistic statement; two stocks with the same country risk (γ) could have different sensitivity to international events because of the nature of the firm's business.

This assumption can be directly tested by verifying the fundamental relation of this specification:

$$\beta_{k_i} = \gamma_{k_i} \beta_k \qquad (37)$$

For each national portfolio the quantity $(\beta_{k_i} - \gamma_{k_i}\beta_k)$ has been estimated and the average absolute value of this deviation for each country compared to the average standard deviation of the risk estimates. It can be seen in Table 8-4

Table 8–4

Test of $\beta_{k_i} = \gamma_{k_i} \beta_k$

Country	Average absolute deviation $\lvert \beta_{k_i} - \gamma_{k_i} \beta_k \rvert$ for portfolios	Average standard deviation of β_{k_i}
France	0.06	0.16
Italy	0.13	0.15
U.K.	0.32[a]	0.14
Germany	0.05	0.16
Holland	0.20[a]	0.09
Switzerland	0.28[a]	0.13
Belgium	0.43[a]	0.12
U.S.A.	0.16	0.16

[a]Larger than 2 standard deviation.

that the deviations from zero are large in many countries. This is especially the case for countries whose market is very internationally oriented (Switzerland, U.K., Belgium, the Netherlands). While these figures are purely indicative and do not allow for decisive conclusions, they suggest a way to improve the specification.

A Multinational Index Model

In our quest for a better understanding of the international capital market structure, we have now considered two extreme stochastic security price processes: a purely international specification and a purely nationalistic specification. While some evidence in support of the IAPM has been presented, it has been shown that both specifications did not satisfactorily describe the international relations between capital markets or stock prices.

Independently of their national risk, stocks might be affected differently by international events. This might be due to the international links of the firm, its foreign subsidiaries, the kind of international competition its products are experiencing, its import-export pattern, and so forth. The final specification to be presented now will attempt to account for these differences, thereby providing a more appropriate framework to test the international asset pricing model.

The Specification

The same international relation between country factors is assumed. However, all securities returns are assumed to be influenced by two factors—the world factor and a purely national factor common to all securities of a country and the ratio of the two coefficients is no more assumed to be fixed (and equal to β_k).

$$\bar{I}_k = \alpha_k + \beta_k(\bar{r}_m - \alpha_m) + \epsilon_k \tag{42}$$

and

$$\bar{r}_{k_i} = \alpha_{k_i} + \beta_{k_i}(\bar{r}_m - \alpha_m) + \gamma_{k_i}\epsilon_k + \eta_{k_i} \tag{43}$$

with the standard assumptions

$$\text{cov}(\epsilon_k, \bar{r}_m) = 0 \qquad\qquad \text{for all } k$$

$$\text{cov}(\eta_{k_i}, \epsilon_k) = \text{cov}(\eta_{k_i}, \bar{r}_m) = 0 \qquad\qquad \text{for all } k, i$$

$$\text{cov}(\epsilon_k, \epsilon_j) = \begin{vmatrix} 0 & \text{if } k \neq j \\ \sigma^2 & \text{if } k = j \end{vmatrix}$$

$$\text{cov}(\eta_{k_i}, \eta_{k'_j}) = \begin{vmatrix} 0 & \text{if } k \neq k' \text{ or } i \neq j \\ \sigma_k^2 & \text{if } k = k' \text{ and } i = j \end{vmatrix}$$

ϵ_k is the residual of the regression of the national index versus the world index. It can be considered as a purely national factor orthogonal to the world factor. Since security prices are assumed to be sensitive in different degrees to national and international influence, it is no more the case that

$$\beta_{k_i} = \gamma_{k_i}\beta_k$$

A Testable Hypothesis

Let us now try to eliminate unobservable expectations from the IAPM equation and get a testable relation between realized return using this specification. We already know that (42) and the IAPM can be combined into (39):

$$\bar{I}_k - R_k = \beta_k(\bar{r}_m - R_m) + \epsilon_k \tag{39}$$

Substituting α_{k_i} and α_m from (43) into the IAPM, we get

$$\tilde{r}_{k_i} - R_k = \beta_{k_i}(\tilde{r}_m - R_m) + \gamma_{k_i}\tilde{\epsilon}_k + \eta_{k_i} \tag{44}$$

replacing ϵ_k by its value in (39):

$$\tilde{r}_{k_i} - R_k = \beta_{k_i}(\tilde{r}_m - R_m) + \gamma_{k_i}'(\tilde{I}_k - R_k) - \gamma_{k_i}\beta_k(\tilde{r}_m - R_m) + \eta_{k_i}$$

or

$$\tilde{r}_{k_i} - R_k = (\beta_{k_i} - \gamma_{k_i}\beta_k)(\tilde{r}_m - R_m) + \gamma_{k_i}(\tilde{I}_k - R_k) + \eta_{k_i}$$

Call $\delta_{k_i} = \beta_{k_i} - \gamma_{k_i}\beta_k$. Then

$$\tilde{r}_{k_i} - R_k = \delta_{k_i}(\tilde{r}_m - R_m) + \gamma_{k_i}(\tilde{I}_i - R_i) + \eta_{k_i} \tag{45}$$

since η_{k_i} is orthogonal to $\tilde{r}_m$ and ϵ_k it is also orthogonal to $\tilde{I}_i$.

It should be noticed that in equation (45) the national factors are not orthogonal to the international factor as in (44). Therefore one should not be surprised to find that the national factors have a nonzero expected value. However, any positive expected return is due to its covariance with the international factor, as it can be seen from equation (39). In the time series regression tests of this model, the results will be unaffected by this transformation since regression coefficients are not changed by a linear combination of the variables. Since the national indices are not highly correlated with the world index, we do not get into serious multicolinearity problems.

This relation is different from equation (41) derived from the "nationalistic" specification, whenever $\beta_{k_i} \neq \gamma_{k_i}\beta_k$. If $\beta_{k_i} > \gamma_{k_i}\beta_k$, the stock is more sensitive to international variations than a typical stock of that country.

This relation will be identical to the single world index model if γ_{k_i} is equal to zero. If γ_{k_i} is positive (as expected), purely national factors have a direct influence on the security prices of that country.

Two steps are necessary to test the international asset pricing model, using this relation:

1. Estimate δ_{k_i} and γ_{k_i}, using returns time series for national portfolios. These estimates $\hat{\delta}_{k_i}$ and $\hat{\gamma}_{k_i}$ can be obtained by running the regression:

$$\tilde{r}_{k_it} = \alpha_{k_i} + \delta_{k_i}\tilde{r}_{mt} + \gamma_{k_i}\tilde{I}_{kt} + \mu_{k_it}$$

2.   Run a cross sectional regression of mean realized excess returns (over the
     mean risk free rate of the country) versus the estimates for international
     and national systematic risk

$$\bar{r}_{k_i} - \bar{R}_k = b_0 + b_1 \hat{\delta}_{k_i} + \sum_{j=1}^{n} a_j \hat{\gamma}_{j_i} + \eta_{k_i}$$

where $\hat{\gamma}_{j_i} = 0$ except for $j = k$.

The theoretical values predicted by the IAPM are:

$$b_0 = 0$$
$$b_1 = \bar{r}_m - \bar{R}_m$$
$$a_1 = \bar{I}_1 - \bar{R}_1$$
.
.
.
$$a_k = \bar{I}_k - \bar{R}_k$$
.
.
.

Time Series Regressions

The 73 national portfolios built previously will be used to test this model.
For each portfolio, its biweekly returns were regressed against the returns on its
national and international indices:

$$\tilde{r}_{k_i t} = \alpha_{k_i} + \delta_{k_i} \tilde{r}_{mt} + \gamma_{k_i} \tilde{I}_{kt} + \tilde{\mu}_{k_i t} \tag{46}$$

The results of those time series regressions are given in Appendix B while
summary statistics are given in Table 8–5. The first set of results give the mean
and the standard deviation of the *sample distribution* (for 73 portfolios) of the
coefficient estimates, their t-statistics, and the R-square of the regressions.

In general the intercept terms, α, are small and not significantly different
from zero (the standard deviation of $t - \alpha$ is only 1.1). Also, it appears clearly
that the explanatory power of the two factors, national and international, is
large. More important, the national factor seems dominant; the average gamma
is equal to 0.94 (with an average t-statistic of 14.2); therefore all stocks do follow

Table 8-5
Summary of Time-series Statistics on α, δ, γ

	Alpha	Delta	Gamma	
Mean	−0.07	0.14	0.94	
St. Dev.	(0.20)	(0.17)	(0.23)	
	t-Alpha	t-Delta	t-Gamma	R**2
Mean	−0.30	1.15	14.2	0.73
St. Dev.	(1.1)	(1.7)	(5.0)	(0.13)
	Abs. Value |delta|	St. Error |delta|	Abs. Value |t-delta|	
Mean	0.18	0.15	1.39	

closely national movements. Again, this result is by no means inconsistent with the international asset pricing model; if the "nationalistic" market structure developed above (see page 79) is an adequate description of the reality, one would expect δ_{k_i} to be zero and all the international effects would be picked through the national factor. Although many δ estimates do not strongly differ from zero, some portfolios might be under strong international influence ($\delta > 0$), some are less dependent on international events ($\delta < 0$), while others are just as sensitive to international influence as a typical stock or the country market as a whole. Therefore no general conclusions can be drawn from the observation of those deltas.

Some insight can be gained by looking at the mean absolute value of δ (rather than its mean). In the last row of Table 8-5, it can be seen that the absolute mean value of δ is 0.18 larger than the mean standard deviation of the estimate 0.15 with an average absolute t-statistic of 1.39. Although these results do not allow us to reject the hypothesis of a "nationalistic" market structure, they do indicate a direct international influence (affecting each stock differently).

Since the stocks in our sample are generally large, internationally oriented companies, it should be expected to find that they are more sensitive to international events than a typical stock of the country. In fact, we do find a predominance of positive δ's.

Cross-Sectional Regressions

Using the estimates obtained in the previous section, we will now run a cross-sectional regression of mean realized excess returns (over the mean risk free rate of the country) versus the estimates for international and national systematic risk. Thus:

$$\bar{r}_{k_i} - \bar{R}_k = b_0 + b_1 \hat{\delta}_{k_i} + \sum_{j=1}^{n} a_j \hat{\gamma}_{j_i} + \eta_{k_i} \tag{47}$$

where $\hat{\gamma}_{j_i} = 0$ except for $j = k$; i.e., it will be zero for all countries except that of the stock. For a portfolio k_i of country k:

$$\bar{r}_{k_i} - \bar{R}_k = b_0 + b_1 \hat{\delta}_{k_i} + a_1 \cdot 0 + \ldots + a_{k-1} \cdot 0 + a_k \hat{\gamma}_{k_i} + \eta_{k_i}$$

This is due to the fact that the international factor δ appears for all stocks, while the national factor γ_{k_i} appears only for stocks of country k. The theoretical value predicted by the IAPM are:

$$b_0 = 0$$

$$b_1 = \bar{r}_m - \bar{R}_m$$

.

.

.

$$a_k = \bar{I}_k - \bar{R}_k$$

.

.

.

Therefore all 73 portfolios will be used to estimate $b_0, b_1, a_1, \ldots, a_n$.

To make sure that the colinearity between the independent variables is not large, the correlation matrix between alpha, delta, and gamma is given in Table 8-6. The correlation between values of γ and δ for all national portfolios is only equal to -0.40. If the test had been performed on equation (44), the multicolinearity would have been a serious problem in the cross-sectional regression since β_{k_i} and γ_{k_i} are strongly correlated.

The cross-sectional results for the period March 1967–April 1971 are given in Table 8-7, along with the theoretical values predicted by the IAPM. The estimated values are in good agreement with the predictions; the standard errors are generally low and the fit is good ($R^2 = 0.78$, with 69 degrees of freedom). However, the constant term is markedly too small (-0.09 instead of zero—i.e., a difference of 2.5 percent annually) and the slope coefficients are generally too large.

Table 8-6
Correlation Matrix of α, δ, γ (Cross-Sectional)

Alpha	Delta	Gamma
1.00	-0.27	-0.33
	1.00	-0.40
		1.00

Table 8-7
**Cross-Sectional Regression Results for 73 National Portfolios
(1967-1971)**

Independent variable	Estimated coefficient	Standard error	Predicted value
C	-0.09	0.06	0
Delta	0.33	0.09	0.23
γ U.K.	0.15	0.06	0.13
γ France	0.45	0.07	0.30
γ Italy	-0.02	0.06	-0.04
γ Germany	0.41	0.07	0.21
γ U.S.A.	0.03	0.05	0.02
$R^2 = 0.785$			

Preliminary Conclusions

The results of the tests performed in Chapters 7 and 8 will be discussed and compared in Chapter 9. It can already be pointed out that stock price movements exhibit a strong dependence on national factors but with an international pricing of risk. Some indication has been given that stocks were not exclusively (and identically) affected by international events through their covariance with the domestic factor but also selectively according to a direct dependence.

Notes

1.   See Friend and Blume [13]; Jacob [19]; and Black, Jensen, and Scholes [3].

9 Conclusions

An intertemporal equilibrium model of the international capital market has been developed in this book under certain assumptions about the capital markets perfection and the consumption behavior of investors. After discussing the underlying framework, some important results have been derived from this international asset pricing model.

Summary and Conclusions

Some "mutual funds theorems" can be derived with important implications for investment policies. The most important of these theorems states that all investors will be indifferent between choosing portfolios from the original assets or from three funds, namely:

1. A portfolio of all stocks hedged against exchange risk (the market portfolio)
2. A portfolio of bonds, speculative in the exchange risk dimension
3. The risk free asset of their own country

This separation theorem implies that exchange risks do not affect investment decisions too strongly. The desired level of risk can be attained by investing in only two mutual funds, identical for everyone. Even with more general assumptions, the separation property holds—although the number and composition of the funds are affected.

From a *practical* point of view, this theory points out that everyone would gain if internationally diversified mutual funds were offered to the public (since investing abroad can be difficult and costly for individuals). In fact the IAPM indicates that a fund with the composition of that first hedged fund (market value weights) would be the only equity portfolio needed by *any* investor to make his investment decisions. A more realistic mutual fund has been suggested by Modigliani; it would be composed of stocks of each country proportionally to the amount invested in the fund by investors of that country. Each investor's share would therefore be protected, to a large degree, against unexpected changes in exchange controls, since the fund could always pay back the investor with his country's stocks.[a]

Risk Pricing Relations

Further, some risk pricing relations have been derived. The international asset pricing model not only brings an international dimension to modern capital theory but also has strong implications for the much debated interest rate theory.

A risk pricing relation can be derived which states that the risk premium of a security over its national risk free rate is proportional to its international systematic risk. The coefficient of proportionality is the risk premium of the world market over a world bond rate.

$$\alpha_i - R_i = \beta_i(\alpha_m - R_m) \tag{16}$$

where

α_i is the expected return on security i (in local currency)

R_i is the interest rate in the country of security i (in local currency)

α_m is the expected return on the world market portfolio (where each component is expressed in its own currency)

R_m is the average interest rate in the world

$\beta_i = \dfrac{\sigma_{im}}{\sigma_m^2}$ is the international systematic risk of security i

The most obvious differences between relation (16) and the capital asset pricing model relation are:

1. The systematic risk is the international systematic risk, involving the covariance of the stock return with the world market portfolio
2. R_i and R_m are, in general, different as it will be seen now

Another set of relations states that the difference between interest rates of

---

[a]The fear of constraints on capital movements, political changes, exchange control is the greatest impediment to widespread foreign investment.

two countries is equal to the expected change of parities between these two countries plus a term depending on exchange risk covariances:

$$R_i - R_n = \mu_{ni} + \frac{\phi_{iw}}{\phi_w{}^2} R_w \qquad (25)$$

In an equilibrium model the difference between interest rates of two countries has to be equal to the coverage rate; therefore the above relations imply that the forward exchange rate is a *biased* estimate of the future exchange rate. This is widely believed but generally for different and conflicting reasons. Here we demonstrate that the spread in interest rate should be equal to the expected change of parity plus a "hedging pressure" term. The close relation of these results with the Habitat theory developed by Modigliani in the national context should be noticed. The direction of the bias depends on the net foreign investment of each country.

While this result is of strong relevance to the exchange risk and interest rate theories, it is very hard to test empirically. This endeavor is left for future times and this book focused on the empirical examination of the risk pricing relation for stocks.

Empirical Testing

The purpose of the empirical part was not only to test the international asset pricing model but also to investigate the international market structure and the relationship between security prices of different countries.

Several stochastic security price processes are consistent with the international asset pricing model, from a single international index model to a very "nationalistic" specification of the market structure. It appears clear that security price movements are strongly affected by national factors. However, stock prices are also influenced by international events, not only through the dependence of the national indices on the international factor but also directly and selectively for each stock.

The tests of the mean return international risk relation generally provide strong support to the international asset pricing model. National markets (i.e., national stock indices) with larger international systematic risk tend to realize on the average larger returns. Similarly the tests conducted under a multinational index specification points towards an international pricing of risk as claimed by the IAPM; the cross-sectional regression results for internationally diversified portfolios lead to the same conclusion. For an international portfolio the national influences get diversified away, and the risk of the portfolio reduces to its (international) systematic risk.

These results are very powerful. They confirm the intuitive feeling that security prices are under strong domestic influence but point strongly towards an international pricing of risk, indicating that the international equity market is probably much more efficient than many think.

The results presented in Chapter 8 show why tests of the capital asset pricing model on the domestic markets ought to give some positive results. However, since the international factor is not directly taken into account, the CAPM is misspecified and the significance of the tests reduced.

Further Research

Several directions of research have been suggested in this book. The results of the international asset pricing model are very powerful; however, since they have been derived under a set of rather restrictive assumptions their robustness should be studied in greater detail by relaxing the assumptions as it has sometimes been done in this book.

An attempt should be made to measure empirically the exchange risks and expectations on change in parities in order to test the relation involving interest rates.

Finally, it would be interesting to explain the selective dependence on the international factor for individual stocks. A multi-industry model (across countries) might be more appropriate than a multinational model which does not take into account the business of the firm and its international characteristics.

Appendixes

Appendix A: The General Case

Let us now consider the most sophisticated model, allowing for nonzero expectations on changes in parity and dependence between the fluctuations in exchange rates and the level of stock prices.

This model is very rich, because it allows for a rather sophisticated description of the international mechanisms while still theoretically and empirically tractable.

The *budget equations* (5) that were established earlier are still valid:

$$\frac{dW^\kappa}{W^\kappa} = \left[R_k + \sum_{i \neq k}^{n} y_i^\kappa (R_i + \mu_{ik} - R_k) + \sum_{i=1}^{n} x_i^\kappa (\alpha_i - R_i + \rho_{ik} \sigma_i \varphi_{ik}) \right] dt$$

$$+ \sum_{i \neq k}^{} y_i^\kappa \varphi_{ik} dq_{ik} + \sum_{i=1}^{n} x_i^\kappa \sigma_i dz_i + \frac{1}{W^\kappa} (Y^\kappa - C^\kappa) dt \qquad (5)$$

As in the previous version, the *optimality conditions* can be derived:

$$0 = J_W^\kappa (R_i + \mu_{ik} - R_k) + W^\kappa J_{WW}^\kappa \left[\sum_{j \neq k} y_j^\kappa \Phi_{ij}^k \right.$$

$$\left. + \sum_{j=1}^{} x^\kappa \rho_{ji} \sigma_j \varphi_{ik} \right] \qquad i \neq k \qquad (26)$$

$$0 = J_W^\kappa (\alpha_i - R_i + \rho_{ik} \sigma_i \varphi_{ik}) + W^\kappa J_{WW}^\kappa \left[\sum_{j=1}^{n} x_j^\kappa \sigma_{ij} \right.$$

$$\left. + \sum_{j \neq k} y_j^\kappa \rho_{ij} \sigma_i \varphi_{jk} \right] \qquad i = 1, 2, \ldots, n \qquad \text{2n-1 equations}$$

In matrix form and with the same notations as before, we get:

99

$$\|R_i + \mu_{ik} - R_k\| = A^{\kappa}(\Phi^k y + P^k x)$$

$$\|\alpha_i - R_i + \rho_{ik}\sigma_i\varphi_{ik}\| = A^{\kappa}(\Sigma x + P^{kT} y) \qquad (27)$$

where

P^k is the covariance matrix between the $(n - 1 x n)$ market and exchange risk

$$P^k = \|\frac{df_{ik}}{f_{ik}} \times \frac{dI_j}{I_j} = p^k_{ij}\|$$

The demands for assets are not separable any more, *and* the left hand sides, Φ^k, and P^k depends on k.

To still get some interesting separation results it is necessary to perform the transformation presented earlier. Taking country n as a reference:

$$p^k_{ij} = \frac{df_{ik}}{f_{ik}} \frac{dI_j}{I_j} = \left(\frac{df_{in}}{f_{in}} - \frac{df_{kn}}{f_{kn}}\right)\frac{dI_j}{I_j} = p^n_{ij} - p^n_{kj}$$

Thus $P^k = H^k P^n = H^k P$.

Then (16) and (17) can be rewritten as:

$$H^k \|R_i + \mu_{in} - R_n\| = A^{\kappa}(H^k \Phi H^{kT} y + H^k Px)$$

$$\|\alpha_i + \rho_{in}\sigma_i\varphi_{in} - R_i\| = \rho_{kn}\varphi_{kn}\sigma_k + A^{\kappa}[\Sigma x + P^T H^{kT} y]$$

and since H^k is inversible,

$$\|R_i + \mu_{in} - R_n\| = A^{\kappa}[\Phi z + Px]$$

$$\|\alpha_i + \rho_{in}\sigma_i\varphi_{in} - R_i\| = \rho_{kn}\varphi_{kn}\sigma_k + A^{\kappa}[\Sigma x + P^T z]$$

Only A^{κ} and $\rho_{kn}\varphi_{kn}\sigma_k$ (same for all i's) depends on k.

Demand Functions

Let us call $G = \|g_{ij}\|$ the inverse matrix of $\left(\sum_P P^T_\Phi\right)$ Then:

$$x_i^\kappa = \frac{1}{A^\kappa} \sum_{j=1}^{n} g_{ij}(\alpha_j + \rho_{jn}\sigma_j\varphi_{jn} - R_j) + \frac{1}{A^\kappa} \sum_{j=1}^{n-1} g_{i,n+j}(R_j + \mu_{jn} - R_n)$$

$$+ \frac{\rho_{kn}}{A^\kappa}\, \varphi_{kn}\sigma_n \sum_{j=1}^{n} g_{ij}$$

.
.
.

$$z_i^\kappa = \frac{1}{A^\kappa} \sum_{j=1}^{n} g_{j,n+i}(\alpha_j + \rho_{jn}\sigma_j\varphi_{jn} - R_j) + \frac{1}{A^\kappa} \sum_{j=1}^{n-1} g_{n+i,n+j}(R_j + \mu_{jn} - R_n)$$

$$+ \frac{\rho_{kn}}{A^\kappa}\, \varphi_{kn}\sigma_k \sum_{j=1}^{n} g_{n+i,j}$$

.
.

$$z_n^\kappa = - \sum_{i=1}^{n-1} z_i^\kappa \tag{28}$$

The subscript i refers to stock I_i; the subscript $n + i$ refers to bond B_i.

As before y_i^κ, the demand for assets of country i is equal to z_i^κ, except for country k where

$$z_i^\kappa = y_i^\kappa - 1$$

The demand functions are of the form

$$a_\kappa c_1(i) + b_\kappa c_2(i) + \ldots$$

This suggests the existence of a four funds theorem whose tedious demonstration will not be given here.

Separation Theorem 3

All investors will be indifferent between choosing portfolios from the original set of assets or from four funds, where a possible choice for those funds is:

1. A portfolio of stocks and bonds whose composition depends only on market expected returns and risks characteristics (including covariances between market and exchange risks)
2. A portfolio of bonds and stocks whose composition depends only on bond returns and exchange risk characteristics (including covariances between exchange and market risks)
3. A third portfolio of stocks and bonds whose composition depends only on covariances and not returns
4. The risk free asset of the investor's country

This theorem is quite different from Separation Theorem 2, both by the addition of a new fund and the composition of the other ones. Looking at the demand function (28), it appears that even Theorem 1 would not hold because a stock investment cannot be perfectly hedged against exchange risk any more; it is not possible to consider a fund free of exchange risk to any investor.

Looking at the demand functions (28), it appears that the results would *not* be modified if one considers all stocks of one country even if their correlations with change in parities are different.

While it is quite impressive to find that only four funds may be used for the investment decision of any investor, the composition of these funds is very complex. Unlike in Theorem 2, where market values (D_i) and net foreign investment $(D_i - W_i)$ were the weights of the risky funds, there is no intuitive explanation for the composition of these three risky funds. Similarly the demand functions are not separable any more and the clearing conditions for bonds and stocks leads to complicated mathematical computations which are not reproduced here. The resulting risk pricing relations are rather complex and not intuitively appealing. Loosely speaking, they indicate a linear relationship between expected returns and covariances with the stock portfolios and the bond portfolios.

Some further research might make these results more appealing.

Appendix B: List of Stocks Used in This Study

U.S.A.

ABJ	ABACUS FUND	ABC	AMER BROADCAST
ABT	ABBOT LABORATORIES	AC	AMER CAN CO
ACF	ACF INDUSTRIES	ACN	AMER CHAIN & CBL
AMT	ACME CLEVELAND CORP	ACS	AMER CRYSTAL SUGAR
ASC	ACME MARKETS, INC	ACY	AMER CYANAMID
ADX	ADAMS EXPRESS CORP	ADC	AMERICAN DISTILLING
ALL	ADAMS-MILLIS CORP	AEP	AMER ELECT & POWER
AIN	ADDRESSO MULTIGRAPH	AHP	AMER HOME PROD
ADL	ADMIRAL CORP	AHS	AMER HOSP SUP
AGG	AGUIRE CORP	AIC	AMER INVEST CO
APD	AIR PRODUCTS & CHEM	AMX	AMER METAL CLIMAX
AN	AIR REDUCTION	AMO	AMER MOTORS CORP
AJ	A J INDUSTRIES	ANG	AMER NATURAL GAS
AGA	ALABAMA GAS CORP	APY	AMER PHOTO EQUIP
AL	ALCAN ALUMINUM	ARD	AMER RESEARCH DEV
Y	ALLEGHANY	AMZ	AMER SEATING CORP
AG	ALLEGHENY LUDLUM	ABG	AMER SHIP BLDG
AYP	ALLEGHENY POWER SYSTEM	AR	AMER SME TG & REFNG
ACD	ALLIED CHEMICAL CORP	ASA	AMER SO AFR INVEST
ADS	ALLIED MILLS INC	AST	AMER STANDARD
ADP	ALLIED PRODUCT	ASR	AMSTAR CORP
ALS	ALLIED STORE	T	AMER TEL & TEL
ASU	ALLIED SUPERMARKETS	A	ANACONDA CO
AH	ALLIS-CHALMERS MFG	AS	ARMCO STEEL CORP
APC	ALPHA PORTLAND CEMENT	ARC	ATLANTIC RICHFIELD CO
AA	ALUMINIUM CO OF AMERICA	BAW	BABCOCK & WILCOX
AGM	AMALGAMATED SUGAR	BCX	BEECH AIRCRAFT
AB	AMBAC INDUSTRIES	BX	BENDIX CORP
AAE	AMERACE ESNA CORP	BS	BETHLEHEM STEEL CORP
AHC	AMERADA HESS CORP	BA	BOEING COMPANY
AMR	AMER. AIRLINES	BND	BOND INDUSTRY
ABA	AMER. BAKERIES	BSE	BOSTON EDISON
AMB	AMER. BRANDS INC		

United Kingdom

DISTILLERS
ASSOCIATED PORTLAND CEMENT
I.C.I.
RANK ORGANISATION
G.U.S.
MARKS & SPENCER
GEC/EE
PLESSEY
THORN ELECTRICAL INDUSTRIES
BEECHAM GROUP
I.C.L.
B.L.M.C.
BOWATER PAPER
REED PAPER
COURTAULDS
BRITISH PETROLEUM
SHELL TRANSPORT (REGISTERED)
TESCO STORES
E.M.I.
ROLLS ROYCE
UNILEVER LTD.
(R.T.Z.)
MARLEY TILE
REDLAND HOLDINGS

RUGBY PORTLAND CEMENT
ALBRIGHT AND WILSON
GLAXO
TUBE INVESTMENTS
HAWKER SIDDELEY
G.K.N.
A.B.FOODS
ASSOCIATED ENGINEERING
B.I.C.C.
FISONS
BRITISH OXIGEN
BURMAH OIL
SLATER WALKER
TUNNEL CEMENT
ENGLISH CHINACLAY
METAL BOX
DUNLOP
LUCAS
GESTETNER
LESNEY PRODUCTS
LAMSON
OZALID
TRUST HOUSES FORTE

France

S.N.P.A.
BANQUE DE L'INDOCHINE
FINANCIERE DE PARIS
CIMENTS LAFARGE
CITROEN
FRANCAISE DES PETROLES
C.G.E.
GALERIES LAFAYETTE
AIR LIQUIDE
MACHINES BULL
MICHELIN

ALSTHOM
T.R.T.
HACHETTE
EUROPE NO 1
SABLIERES DE LA SEINE
EUROPEENNE DE BRASSERIES
CLUB MEDITERRANEE
SOMMER
PATERNELLE R.D. (LA)
PATERNELLE VIE
GERVAIS-DANONE

PECHINEY
PEUGEOT
PRINTEMPS (AU)
REDOUTE (LA)
RHONE-POULENC
CIE ST GOBAIN-PONT-A-MOUSSON
THOMSON BRANDT
UGINE KUHLMANN
USINOR
WENDEL (DE)
BOUSSOIS SOUCHON NEUVESEL
SUEZ
SAGEM
ERICSSON (FRANCE)
TELECOMMUNICATIONS (S.A. DE)
SIGNAUX
UNION DE CREDIT POUR LE BATI
NICKEL (LE)
PENARROYA
AUXILIAIRE D'ENTREPRISES
C.S.F.
ELECTRO-MECANIQUE

MOET ET CHANDON
LOCABAIL
COMPAGNIE BANCAIRE
CREDIT NATIONAL
SOVAC
EVIAN
PERRIER
NOUVELLES GALERIES
PARIS-FRANCE
CREUSOT (LE)
ROUSSEL UCLAF
PATERNELLE S.A. (LA)
FIVES LILLE CAIL
U.T.A.
RADIOTECHNIQUE (LA)
OREAL (L')
LOCAFRANCE
L.M.T.
MATRA
SCHNEIDER
C.I.T.
TELEMECANIQUE ELECTRIQUE

Germany

A.E.G.
ALLIANZ VERSICHERUNG
B.A.S.F.
BAYER
DAIMLER-BENZ
DEMAG
DEUTSCHE BANK
DEGUSSA
DRESDNER BANK
FARBWEPKE HOECHST
HOESCH
KARSTADT
KAUFHOF
K.H.C.
LUFTHANSA

R.W.E.
SCHERING
SIEMENS A.G.
AUGUST THYSSEN-HUTTE
VOLKSWAGEN
BEIERSDORF
B.B.C. (MANNHEIM)
VEBA
G.H.H.
VARTA
HOCHTIEF
HOLZMANN
METALLGESELLSCHAFT
BAYERISCHE VEREINSBANK
BAYER HYPOTHEKEN BANK

Germany (cont.)

M.A.N.	B-M-W
MUNCHENER RUCKVERSICHERUNG	DYCKERHOFF ZEMENT
NECKERMANN	HEIDELBERG ZEMENT
PREUSSAG	HORTEN

Italy

ANIC	CENTRALE (LA)
ASSICURAZIONI GENERALI	DALMINE
BREDA FINANZIARA	MONTE AMIATA
MONTECATINI EDISON	C.I.G.A.
CARLO ERBA	MAGNETI MARELLI
FIAT (ORDINARY)	PIERREL S.P.A.
GENERALE IMMOBILIARE	MIRA LANZA
ITALSIDER	BASTOGI
ERCOLE MARELLI	CERAMICA POZZI
ITALCEMENTI	MONDADORI
MOTTA	CONDOTTE D'ACQUA
OLIVETTI	S.I.P.
PIRELLI S.P.A.	S.T.E.T.
RINASCENTE (LA)	TORO ASSICURAZINCNI
SNIA VISCOSA	CEMENTIR
FINSIDER	ALITALIA
MEDIOBANCA	

Belgium

E.B.E.S.	ARBED
INNO-B.M.	COCKERILL-DUGREE
INTERCOM	G.B.ENTREPRISES
ROYALE BELGE (LA)	KREDIETBANK
PETROFINA	C B R
GEVAERT	SOLVAY
STE GENERALE DE BELGIQUE	HOBOKEN
STE GENERALE DE BANQUE	TRACTION ET ELECTRICITE
BANQUE DE BRUXELLES	

Netherlands

A K Z O	AMRO BANK
HOOGOVENS	ALGEMENE BANK

NATIONALE NEDERLANDEN   GIST BROCADES
PHILIPS   VAN DER GRINTEN
ROYAL DUTCH   BUHRMANN–TETTERODE
K.L.M.   D.R.U.
UNILEVER N.V.   MIDDENSTANDSBANK
ALBERT HEIJN   SCHOLTEN HONIG
HEINEKEN   SLAVENBURG'S BANK
BIJENKORF   VAN NELLE
FOKKER   BREDERO
V.M.F.   PAKHOED HOLDING
ELSEVIER   NAARDEN

Switzerland

HOFFMANN–LA ROCHE (REG. SHARE)
SWISSAIR (BEARER)
NESTLE (REGISTERED SHARES)
CIBA–GEIGY (HIS'T CIBA) (BEARER)
STE DE BANQUE SUISSE
CREDIT SUISSE
ALUMINIUM SUISSE (REG. SHARE)
B.B.C. (SUISSE)
CIBA–GEIGY (HIS'T CIBA) (REG. SHARE)
CIBA–GEIGY (HIS'T GEIGY) (REG. SHARE)
CIBA–GEIGY (HIS'T GEIGY) (BEARER)
NESTLE (BEARER)
HOFFMANN–LA ROCHE (P.S.C.)
SWISSAIR (REGISTERED)
SULZER (REGISTERED SHARES)
SULZER (PART CERT.)
ALUMINIUM SUISSE (BEARER)
UNION DE BANQUES SUISSES
CIBA–GEIGY (HIS'T GEIGY)
URSINA FRANCK–A6

Appendix C: Time Series Regression of 76 National Portfolios

ALPHA	S.ER. ALPHA	DELTA	S.ER. DELTA	GAMMA	S.ER. GAMMA	R**2
0.240	0.155	0.044	0.116	1.216	0.050	0.90
-0.040	0.190	0.316	0.135	0.988	0.057	0.84
0.120	0.160	0.158	0.117	0.819	0.050	0.82
0.000	0.000	0.404	0.148	0.649	0.063	0.68
0.100	0.122	0.178	0.095	1.105	0.040	0.92
0.050	0.128	0.277	0.103	0.736	0.043	0.83
0.090	0.132	0.124	0.100	1.148	0.042	0.92
0.020	0.182	0.228	0.104	1.049	0.044	0.90
0.010	0.111	0.335	0.111	0.947	0.047	0.88
0.120	0.148	0.220	0.109	0.868	0.046	0.85
0.120	0.138	0.246	0.101	0.757	0.043	0.84
0.040	0.154	0.251	0.110	0.690	0.047	0.79
0.120	0.200	0.092	0.153	1.060	0.071	0.76
0.020	0.133	-0.037	0.122	0.893	0.057	0.76
-0.100	0.179	0.032	0.131	0.886	0.061	0.74
0.100	0.179	0.016	0.130	0.854	0.060	0.73
0.210	0.193	-0.175	0.146	0.622	0.067	0.50
0.070	0.140	0.024	0.113	0.965	0.051	0.83
0.060	0.136	-0.037	0.108	0.789	0.050	0.77
0.090	0.187	0.040	0.141	1.054	0.065	0.78
0.080	0.160	0.069	0.117	0.981	0.055	0.82
0.040	0.167	-0.030	0.115	0.919	0.053	0.80
0.030	0.167	0.032	0.121	0.844	0.056	0.76
-0.080	0.160	-0.042	0.127	0.909	0.058	0.76
-0.010	0.167	0.016	0.124	0.911	0.059	0.76
-0.010	0.111	-0.020	0.125	0.920	0.058	0.77
0.080	0.160	0.048	0.121	0.798	0.056	0.73
0.150	0.170	-0.051	0.131	0.743	0.060	0.66
0.180	0.176	-0.087	0.134	0.638	0.061	0.57
-0.240	0.162	0.297	0.124	0.975	0.071	0.75

ALPHA	S.ER. ALPHA	DELTA	S.ER. DELTA	GAMMA	S.ER. GAMMA	R**2
0.060	0.120	0.142	0.091	1.002	0.052	0.84
-0.060	0.146	0.086	0.103	0.777	0.060	0.70
-0.130	0.134	0.246	0.104	0.970	0.060	0.80
-0.030	0.103	0.112	0.077	0.872	0.044	0.85
-0.130	0.134	0.246	0.104	0.970	0.060	0.80
-0.030	0.120	0.143	0.075	0.991	0.043	0.88
0.050	0.106	0.099	0.086	1.001	0.049	0.85
-0.030	0.103	0.112	0.077	0.872	0.044	0.85
-0.080	0.099	0.178	0.076	0.923	0.044	0.87
-0.010	0.111	-0.119	0.135	1.148	0.075	0.77
0.040	0.167	-0.078	0.124	1.088	0.069	0.79
0.170	0.187	-0.011	0.154	1.021	0.085	0.69
0.010	0.200	-0.150	0.125	1.130	0.070	0.79
0.130	0.169	0.018	0.140	1.036	0.077	0.74
-0.030	0.136	-0.143	0.127	1.116	0.071	0.78
0.030	0.143	-0.094	0.115	1.098	0.064	0.81
0.120	0.143	-0.082	0.113	1.073	0.063	0.81
0.130	0.155	-0.043	0.131	1.051	0.073	0.76
0.170	0.183	-0.012	0.156	1.031	0.085	0.70
0.030	0.150	0.557	0.097	0.466	0.085	0.50
0.050	0.128	0.646	0.096	0.253	0.085	0.44
0.040	0.121	0.601	0.076	0.358	0.067	0.58
-0.320	0.165	0.539	0.153	0.703	0.091	0.70
-0.080	0.138	0.291	0.132	0.604	0.078	0.65
-0.200	0.109	0.413	0.100	0.653	0.060	0.81
0.020	0.222	0.154	0.183	1.015	0.092	0.70
-0.250	0.214	0.252	0.185	0.726	0.094	0.57
-0.110	0.186	0.228	0.162	0.855	0.082	0.69
-0.150	0.253	0.057	0.204	1.486	0.119	0.70
-0.100	0.232	0.279	0.185	1.333	0.110	0.72
-0.100	0.231	0.082	0.185	1.229	0.110	0.66
-0.250	0.218	0.201	0.174	1.074	0.103	0.65
0.030	0.274	0.018	0.221	0.731	0.129	0.33
0.040	0.278	0.409	0.223	0.649	0.132	0.36
-0.140	0.256	0.137	0.204	1.480	0.121	0.70
-0.070	0.222	0.384	0.179	1.283	0.106	0.73

ALPHA	S.ER. ALPHA	DELTA	S.ER. DELTA	GAMMA	S.ER. GAMMA	R**2
0.010	0.220	0.218	0.176	1.257	0.104	0.71
-0.070	0.194	0.227	0.152	1.228	0.090	0.76
-0.140	0.182	0.115	0.147	1.130	0.087	0.73
-0.270	0.207	0.186	0.163	1.184	0.097	0.71
-0.180	0.171	0.072	0.138	1.093	0.081	0.74
-0.080	0.230	0.064	0.183	1.044	0.108	0.59
0.020	0.239	0.019	0.190	0.851	0.112	0.47
0.010	0.257	0.154	0.202	0.739	0.120	0.40
0.000	0.212	0.312	0.167	0.646	0.099	0.47
-0.090	0.138	0.173	0.110	1.089	0.065	0.82

Bibliography

1. Agmon, T., "Interrelations Among Equity Markets," unpublished Ph.D. thesis, University of Chicago, May 1971.
2. Black, F., "Capital Market Equilibrium with Restricted Borrowing," *Journal of Business,* July 1972.
3. Black, F., Jensen, M., Scholes, M., "The Capital Asset Pricing Model: Some Empirical Tests," in *Studies of the Theory of Capital Markets,* Jensen (Ed.), New York: Praeger, 1972.
4. Blume, M., "The Assessment of Portfolio Performance," unpublished Ph.D. thesis, University of Chicago, 1968.
5. Conway, "An Examination of the Robustness and Stability of the Beta Coefficient as a Measure of Systematic Risk in Managed Portfolio," unpublished Master's thesis, Massachusetts Institute of Technology, June 1972.
6. Cootner, P. (Ed.), *The Random Character of Stock Prices,* Cambridge, Mass.: MIT Press, 1967.
7. Dryden, M., "Share Price Movements: A Markovian Approach," *Journal of Finance,* March 1969, pp. 49-61.
8. EEC, "The Development of a European Capital Market," European Economic Community, Brussels, 1966.
9. EEC, "Algemeine Statistik," Statistical Office of the European Economic Community, various issues.
10. Fama, E., "The Behavior of Stock Market Prices," *Journal of Business,* January 1965, pp. 34-105.
11. Fama, E., "Tomorrow on the New York Stock Exchange," *Journal of Business,* July 1965, pp. 285-299.
12. Fama, E., "Risk, Return and Equilibrium: Some Clarifying Comments," *Journal of Finance,* March 1968, pp. 29-40.
13. Friend, I., and Blume, M., "Measurement of Portfolio Performance Under Uncertainty," *American Economic Review,* September 1970.
14. Grubel, H. G., *Forward Exchange, Speculation and the International Flow of Capital,* Palo Alto: Stanford University Press, 1966.
15. Grubel, H. G., "Internationally Diversified Portfolios: Welfare Gains and Capital Flows," *American Economic Review,* December 1968, pp. 1299-1314.
16. Grubel, H. G., and Fadner, K., "The Interdependence of International Equity Markets," *Journal of Finance,* March 1971, pp. 89-94.
17. IMF, *International Monetary Funds Statistics,* various issues.
18. IMF, "Annual Report on Exchange Restrictions," International Monetary Fund, 1972.
19. Jacob, N., "The Measurement of Systematic Risk for Securities and Portfolios: Some Empirical Results," *Journal of Financial & Quantitative Analysis,* March 1971, pp. 815-834.
20. Jensen, M. C. (Ed.), *Studies in the Theory of Capital Markets,* New York: Praeger, 1972.
21. Kendall, M. G., "The Analysis of Economic Time Series: Part I, Prices,"

Journal of the Royal Statistical Society, March–April 1953, Vol. 7, pp. 145–173.

22. Kindleberger, C. P., *International Economics,* Irwin Series, Homewood, Illinois, 1968.

23. King, B.F., "Market and Industry Factors in Stock Price Behavior," *Journal of Business,* January 1966, pp. 139–190.

24. Levy, H., and Sarnat, M., "International Diversification of Investment Portfolios," *American Economic Review,* September 1970, pp. 668–675.

25. Lintner, "Security Prices, Risk, and Maximal Gains from Diversification," *Journal of Finance,* December 1965, pp. 587–615.

26. Malinvaud, E., *Statistical Methods of Econometrics* (2nd ed.), Amsterdam: North-Holland Publishers, 1970.

27. Markowitz, H., *Portfolio Selection, Efficient Diversification of Investments,* New York: Wiley, 1959.

28. Merton, R. C., "Optimum Consumption and Portfolio Rules in Continuous-Time Model," *Journal of Economic Theory 3,* December 1971.

29. Merton, R. C., "An Intertemporal Capital Asset Pricing Model," MIT Working Paper #588-72, February 1972.

30. Modigliani, F., Pogue, G. A., Scholes, M. S., Solnik, B. H., "Efficiency of European Capital Markets and Comparison with the American Market," *Proceedings of the 1st International Congress on Stock Exchanges,* Milan, 1972.

31. Mossin, J., "Equilibrium in a Capital Asset Market," *Econometrica,* October 1966, pp. 768–783.

32. OECD, "Capital Market Study," Committee for Invisible Transactions, OECD publication, August 1967.

33. OECD, "The Business and Industry Advisory Committee Report on Capital Markets and Capital Movements," Brussels, March 1969.

34. OECD, "Code of Liberalization of Capital Movements," Paris, 1970.

35. Sharpe, W. F., "A Simplified Model for Portfolio Analysis," *Management Science,* January 1963, pp. 277–293.

36. Sharpe, W. F., "Capital Asset Prices: A Theory of Market Equilibrium Under Conditions of Risk," *Journal of Finance,* September 1964, pp. 425–442.

37. Sharpe, W. F., "Linear Programming Algorithm for Mutual Fund Portfolio Selection," *Management Science,* March 1967, pp. 499–510.

38. Sharpe, W. F., *Portfolio Theory and Capital Markets,* New York: McGraw-Hill, 1970.

39. Solnik, B. H., "The Behavior of European Stock Prices," MIT Working Paper #581-71, Sloan School of Management, January 1972.

40. Templeman, D., "Liberalization of Portfolio Investment and the Development of Securities Markets in the OECD," *Journal of World Trade Law,* 1972.

41. Theil, H., and Leenders, C. T., "Tomorrow on the Amsterdam Stock Exchange," *Journal of Business,* July 1965, pp. 277–284.

About the Author

Bruno H. Solnik is Assistant Professor of Finance at the Graduate School of Business, Stanford University. He previously taught at the University of Paris where he received a doctorate in Applied Economics. He also holds a PhD from the Massachusetts Institute of Technology. Professor Solnik is the author of numerous professional articles and a book on *Linear Programming for Management.*